JANE AUSTEN'S
GARDEN

Also by Molly Williams

The Junior Plant Lover's Handbook: A Green-Thumb Guide for Kids

How to Speak Flower: A Kid's Guide to Buds, Blooms, and Blossoms

Taming the Potted Beast: The Strange and Sensational History of the Not-So-Humble Houseplant

Killer Plants: Growing and Caring for Flytraps, Pitcher Plants, and Other Deadly Flora

JANE AUSTEN'S
GARDEN

A Botanical Tour of the Classic Novels

MOLLY WILLIAMS

illustrated by
JESSICA ROUX

Andrews McMeel
PUBLISHING®

Andrews McMeel Publishing
a division of Andrews McMeel Universal
1130 Walnut Street, Kansas City, Missouri 64106

www.andrewsmcmeel.com

25 26 27 28 29 POA 10 9 8 7 6 5 4 3 2 1

ISBN: 978-1-5248-8637-0

Library of Congress Control Number: 2024944200

Editor: Melissa R. Zahorsky
Art Director: Holly Swayne
Production Editor: Elizabeth A. Garcia
Production Manager: Julie Skalla

ATTENTION: SCHOOLS AND BUSINESSES
Andrews McMeel books are available at quantity discounts with bulk purchase for
educational, business, or sales promotional use. For information, please e-mail the
Andrews McMeel Publishing Special Sales Department: sales@andrewsmcmeel.com.

For Mom, in honor of her love for Colonel Brandon and Mr. Darcy;
and for Dad, who taught me to love the woods

CONTENTS

Introduction:
WELCOME
TO THE
GARDEN

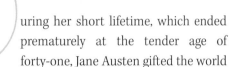uring her short lifetime, which ended prematurely at the tender age of forty-one, Jane Austen gifted the world with six timeless novels, each bearing the indelible imprint of her literary genius. Jane's legacy transcends the passage of time, firmly placing her among the revered pantheon of literary luminaries.

Jane was a remarkable trailblazer, fearlessly navigating new territory by writing about women at a time when such endeavors were uncommon. Despite the prevailing norms of her time, she penned brilliant, enduring novels. However, like many other female authors of the time, she did so anonymously to avoid public scorn. Her first four novels, *Sense and Sensibility* (1811), *Pride and Prejudice* (1813), *Mansfield Park* (1814), and *Emma* (1815), were published without even a pen name on the cover. The first simply read "BY A LADY," and the following three were unattributed as well, only indicating that the novels were all written by the same author. Jane's two remaining novels—*Northanger Abbey* and *Persuasion*—were published posthumously in her name.

Jane's timeless works have served as a wellspring of inspiration for other writers and creators, leading to literary extensions of all kinds, including sequels, prequels, films, and plays, from the BBC's faithful television miniseries *Pride and Prejudice* (1995) to the bestselling *Pride and Prejudice and Zombies* by Seth Grahame-Smith, a horror-comedy novel that combines elements of *Pride and Prejudice* with a zombie apocalypse. There's also the teen-favorite movie *Clueless,* a contemporary retelling of *Emma* that turns Bath into Beverly Hills and follows the stylish and clever Cher Horowitz as she experiences high school life and romance alongside her friends.

Numerous festivals, clubs, and societies pay homage to Jane's legacy, ranging from the yearly Jane Austen Festival in Bath to the Jane Austen Societies in the United Kingdom and North America. Her name alone is now a byword for wit, social observation, and insight into women's lives in the late eighteenth and early nineteenth centuries. Jane is celebrated as a keen social commentator, comic genius, and writer of unparalleled popularity. These are remarkable achievements for the younger daughter of a country rector who completed her formal education at eleven and was never publicly acknowledged as a writer during her lifetime.

Jane Austen's influence continues to grow and flourish, calling to mind her vivid descriptions of nature, like the lush greenery of hedgerows and shrubberies she portrays in her books. As an avid admirer of gardens and green landscapes, my own experiences seamlessly intertwine with her narratives, forging a connection between her natural world and mine. Revisiting her novels feels akin to wandering through my mother's garden, each visit revealing fresh discoveries.

I have always had a fascination with plants and reading. My mother is a flower farmer with an exemplary work ethic and vast knowledge. She taught me how to plant bulbs, tend to houseplants, and cut flowers in the morning before the sun is high— and also how to appreciate a luscious period drama. One of the first books I begged my parents to buy me was a mass-market edition of *Pride and Prejudice*. It's still on my bookshelf, tattered and yellowed from sitting on windowsills throughout the many discretionary moves of my early twenties. Jane's novels continue to transport me each time I page through them. Like old friends, they reveal something new to me each time I visit—which, of course, is how we ended up here, together.

Readers of Jane's novels, like myself, know that the experience of being outdoors, engulfed in nature, is a substantial theme throughout her work. In her fictional worlds, she crafts vast estates with sweeping parklands, quaint cottage gardens, and solitary potted plants. Jane helps readers explore real places, like Box Hill in *Emma*, and fictional locations, like the garden and orchard of Hunsford Parsonage in *Pride and Prejudice* and the woods of *Sense and Sensibility*'s Barton Park. Jane also highlights both wild and tame plants that could be found along the shrubberies and within parklands, and cultivated fruits, like pineapples, strawberries, and apricots. In minute detail, she describes floral conservatories, lawns, and formal landscaping—all of which contribute meaningfully to the lives of her heroines.

Gardens and outdoor spaces play a pivotal role in Jane's novels, not only because they work fabulously as literary devices but also because Jane loved being outdoors as much as her characters did. In the surviving letter to her sister, Cassandra, from December 1798, Jane wrote of enjoying a chilly walk while staying at Godmersham Park in Kent:

I enjoyed the hard black frosts of last week very much, and one day while they lasted walked to Deane by myself. I do not know that I ever did such a thing in my life before.

Within Jane's fictional gardens, she provides her heroines spaces to evade their families, talk privately with friends, and stage secret rendezvous. Among these escapes are Mr. Rushworth's old-fashioned garden in *Mansfield Park,* the expansive kitchen gardens at *Northanger Abbey,* and Mr. Collins's quaint parsonage garden in *Pride and Prejudice.* Jane's acres of towering shrubbery, roaming wildernesses, and gravel garden paths are conveyed as vividly as her characters.

There are innumerable horticulture and landscape design references in Jane's works, but what images do those references conjure for the modern reader? In *Mansfield Park,* when Fanny Price seeks "a breeze of mental strength" from her geraniums, does today's reader see her bent over a potted flower with big red blooms atop stalks? Or are these geraniums the daintier scented cultivars that were common during the Georgian era? And in *Emma,* when the outdoor partygoers at Donwell Abbey seek relief in the shade of "a broad short avenue of limes," do we picture shrubby citrus trees heavy with fruit or a row of towering European lindens? In Jane's era, these references would've been easily recognizable by her readers, limited as they were to England and Europe. Today, however, terms like "lime" and "geranium" are confused by our much broader frame of reference. I hope to unravel that confusion, offering a more accurate picture of Jane's landscapes and world.

Whether you're an Austen fan, Regency buff, plant enthusiast, or—like me—all three, there's plenty here for you. Step into *Jane Austen's Garden* and enjoy the delightful melding of literary exploration and historical yet practical gardening wisdom. Lose yourself in the lush landscapes that stirred Jane's imagination and uncover the captivating tales behind the botanical marvels of the Regency era. Dive into DIY gardening projects with "Cultivated by Jane," sections that transport you to Austen's era to plan and plant a kitchen garden, make lavender water, create Regency tablescapes, and much more.

But don't be fooled—this book isn't solely for literature lovers. It's a lively and approachable companion for anyone who finds solace and joy in gardens and greenery. All you need is an open mind—and maybe a tattered copy of *Pride and Prejudice*—and you'll be ready for a delightful journey.

A NOTE FROM
THE AUTHOR

My intention for this book was to create a compendium
of Regency-era horticultural references that Jane Austen
included in her major novels. To help readers locate the references as they appear in the novels, the title of each entry
reflects the nomenclature Jane used, even when it differs
from what is common today. (For example: The reader will
find information about pelargoniums under the entry titled
"Geranium.") Additionally, the Austen scholar will notice
that I've left out references to *Juvenilia* and Jane's other
minor works, like *Lady Susan* and *Sanditon*. Instead, I chose
to concentrate on her most famed and accessible storytelling. I also chose "England" as a geographical reference rather
than Great Britain or the United Kingdom. My focus is on
the geography and topography that Jane would have written about, primarily the south of England, and not the entire
United Kingdom or Great Britain as we know it today.

JANE AND THE REGENCY ERA: A TIMELINE

1714

After the death of Queen Anne, George I inherits the British throne and begins the Georgian era.

1716

Lancelot "Capability" Brown is born in Northumberland.

JUNE 11, 1727

George I dies, and George II takes the throne.

1750s

Capability Brown starts work on the gardens at Chatsworth House.

OCTOBER 25, 1760

George II dies, and his grandson, George III, becomes king.

1763

Capability Brown starts work on the Blenheim Palace gardens.

DECEMBER 16, 1775

Jane is born in Steventon, Hampshire, England.

1783

Britain surrenders the American colonies. Capability Brown dies.

1797

Jane finishes the initial draft of *First Impressions*, which eventually becomes *Pride and Prejudice*.

1798

Jane starts writing *Susan*, which later becomes *Northanger Abbey*.

MAY 1801

The Austen family leaves Steventon and moves to Bath.

1805

Jane's father dies quickly from an unknown illness. The brothers agree to support their mother and sisters financially, but the three women are forced to move from rental to rental. Jane stops writing.

1806

Jane, along with her mother and sister, moves to Southampton to live with her brother Francis.

1809

Jane's brother Edward offers his six-bedroom cottage in Chawton, part of his estate, as a permanent home for Jane, her mother, and her sister.

1811

Sense and Sensibility is published anonymously, the attribution reading "BY A LADY." The Regency period officially begins after George III falls to mental illness. His son George (later George IV) begins his rule as regent.

1813

First Impressions is published as *Pride and Prejudice.*

1814

Mansfield Park is published. Jane starts writing *Emma* and finishes it in 1815.

JUNE 18, 1815

The Battle of Waterloo takes place on June 18, effectively ending the Napoleonic Wars.

1816

Jane becomes ill but ignores her symptoms and continues writing. *Emma* is published.

1817

In April, Jane is confined to her sickbed. In May, Jane and Cassandra move to Winchester to be near Jane's doctor.

JULY 18, 1817

Jane dies in the morning in Winchester. She is buried at Winchester Cathedral.

DECEMBER 1817

Northanger Abbey and *Persuasion* are published under Jane's full name, revealing her as the author of all her previously published works.

THE
FLOWER
GARDEN

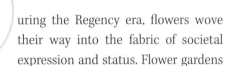uring the Regency era, flowers wove their way into the fabric of societal expression and status. Flower gardens within the estates of the elite stood as living testaments to wealth, taste, and cultural refinement. These carefully cultivated landscapes, influenced by the Romantic movement, were designed to be more than just visually appealing; they were a symphony of colors and fragrances orchestrated to display the sophistication of those who owned them.

Regency flower gardens, often sprawling across expansive estates, became show-cases of botanical variety. Roses, tulips, dahlias, and hyacinths were carefully chosen for their visual appeal and symbolic significance. The cultivation of exotic and rare spe-cies added an extra layer of exclusivity, turning these gardens into living canvases that reflected the tastes of the elite. Skilled gardeners and horticulturists were employed to maintain these outdoor sanctuaries, contributing to the overall refinement of the landscape.

Many of these flowers became powerful symbols of social status. Possessing an extensive, well-tended garden wasn't just about showcasing a love for nature; it was a statement of wealth and a testament to refined cultural sensibilities. Those with the means to curate such gardens exhibited their financial prowess and demonstrated appreciation for nature's artistry.

Floriography, or the language of flowers, added a layer of sophistication to this status-driven floral culture. Exchanging posy bouquets, little flower arrangements often tied with silk ribbons, became a subtle form of communication. Roses, with their varied colors, could convey sentiments of love and passion, while lilies symbolized purity, and violets, modesty. The ability to navigate this coded language reflected cultural refine-ment and social acumen.

Public spaces, such as parks and promenades, were transformed into floral dis-plays, creating opportunities for the elite to showcase not only their fashionable attire but also their connection to nature. Promenading through these carefully curated flower arrangements became a social event where individuals could engage in leisurely strolls, appreciating both the botanical beauty and each other's company.

JANE'S LIFE AND LEGACY

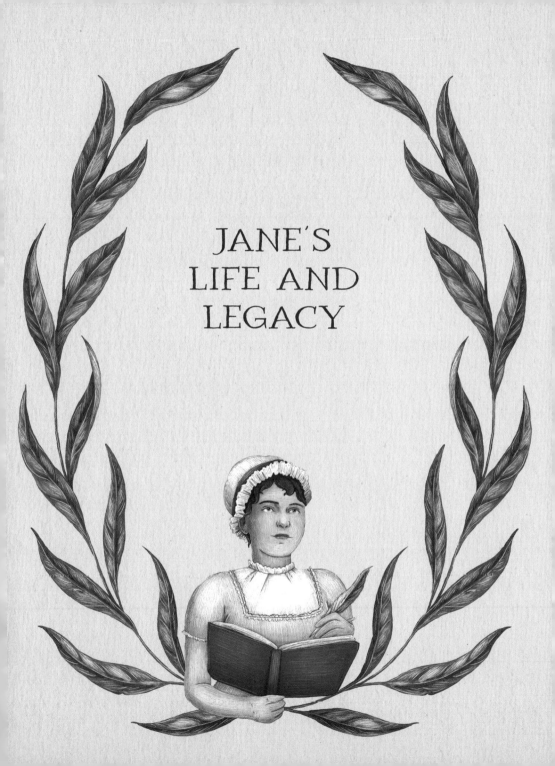

*J*ane Austen was born on December 16, 1775, in Steventon, Hampshire, England, the seventh of eight children to Reverend George and Cassandra Austen. Raised in a large family that prized creativity, the Austen children received an enriching education under the open-minded tutelage of their father. Entertainment in the form of family plays became a cherished pastime, sparking Jane's passion for storytelling.

At the age of seven, Jane was sent with her older sister, Cassandra, to boarding school for a formal education. After returning to Steventon, her father and brothers assumed responsibility for her education, and Jane's burgeoning talent for writing found fertile ground in Reverend Austen's robust library. Well acquainted with social life due to her father's role as a rector, Jane embarked on frequent travels with her family. These experiences—from nearby villages to bustling cities, like Bath and London—laid the foundation for characters and settings in her future works.

In the 1790s, Jane explored experimental short comedies and plays, eventually forming the stories that became *Sense and Sensibility*. Despite personal challenges, including a brief, thwarted romance in 1795 with former neighbor and family friend Tom Lefroy, she persevered in her writing journey. In 1797, she penned *First Impressions*, which she later refined into *Pride and Prejudice*. The early 1800s brought personal and professional changes—her father's retirement, an unexpected proposal (which Jane refused), and a move to Bath.

Following her father's death in 1805, Jane, her mother, and Cassandra experienced multiple relocations before settling in Chawton. With renewed vigor, Jane resumed her work. The successful, albeit anonymous, publication of *Sense and Sensibility* in 1811 was followed by *Pride and Prejudice, Mansfield Park,* and later by *Emma*.

However, by 1816, Jane's health significantly declined. Despite her family's insistence that she seek medical help, she continued to work and succumbed to illness in Winchester on July 18, 1817. She was just forty-one years old.

Posthumously, her siblings Henry and Cassandra had *Northanger Abbey* and *Persuasion* published under her full name, thus revealing Jane as the author of all her previously published works.

Jane's illness and cause of death have been widely argued. For a very long time, it was thought Jane died of complications related to tuberculosis, Addison's disease, or cancer, such as Hodgkin's lymphoma. The most controversial hypothesis came in 2017, when scholars at the British Library revealed a theory dating to 2011 that Jane had been poisoned to death with arsenic. The theory pointed to another popular belief: that Jane had cataracts and suffered deteriorating vision leading up to her death. While it's widely understood today that arsenic causes cataracts and that many medicines during the nineteenth century contained the poison, this theory of Jane's death should be broached with caution. Yes, Jane owned spectacles—in fact, the British Library has many of her effects in its collection and has shared photos of Jane's glasses alongside her portable writing desk. Both items can be seen on display at the library in London. But were the glasses prescribed for cataracts? Did she use them at all, or were they just an accessory? It's impossible to know.

After Jane's death, her literary legacy endured and grew exponentially. Her novels continue to captivate readers, transcending generations and cultures. Her astute social commentary, sharp wit, and timeless characters secured her place as one of the most beloved authors in English literature.

CULTIVATING JANE

Craft Faux Flowers

Step back in time to the lavish and refined world of Jane's Regency, where craftsmanship and delicate aesthetics defined every aspect of life.

During the eighteenth and early nineteenth centuries, artificial flowers adorned the homes and garments of women all over, reflecting a penchant for elegance and sophistication. The use of thin fabric and wax was a hallmark of this period, allowing artisans to produce flowers that were both durable and remarkably lifelike.

These instructions will take you through the simple steps of creating your own faux wax flowers. As you grow more confident in your skills—which might take a few tries to perfect—experiment with different flower varieties, hues, and arrangements to craft a stunning bouquet that pays homage to historical craftsmanship.

YIELD: APPROXIMATELY 24 MEDIUM-SIZED FLOWERS

MATERIALS

Petal Templates

Create templates for the petals that match the shape of the flower type you want to create. You can print predesigned shapes you find online or freehand sketch them onto paper. Cut them out and use them to trace the shape onto the fabric.

Thin Fabric (3 to 5 yards)

Choose a fabric with a fine weave and natural drape, such as muslin or silk organza. The fabric should readily absorb wax and retain its shape after coating. But any fabric will do in a pinch!

Fabric Scissors

Your fabric scissors should be sharp for clean and precise cutting.

Wire Cutters

Use these to cut your floral wire. Do not use your fabric shears, as the wire will quickly dull the blades!

Floral Wire (approximately 120 yards)

Choose thin, flexible floral wire for the stems. The wire provides support and allows for shaping the flowers.

Beeswax or Paraffin Wax (2 pounds)

Beeswax offers a natural touch and a subtle fragrance. It was often used during the Regency era in middle- and upper-class homes as an improvement over tallow. Paraffin wax, which became popular during the 1850s, is a petroleum-based alternative that may be easier to find and more affordable.

Double Boiler or Microwave-Safe Bowl

Use a double boiler to melt the wax gently, or opt for microwaving in a microwave-safe bowl.

Small Tongs or Tweezers (optional)

To avoid burning your fingers, you can use tongs or tweezers to dip your fabric petals in the hot wax.

Paintbrush

Select a small, fine-bristled paintbrush for precise wax application. This tool is essential for coating the fabric petals evenly.

Floral Stamens (1 pack, typically sold in packs of 140)

Commercially made floral stamens or handmade clusters using fine wires and tiny beads serve as the central element of the flower.

Watercolor Paint (optional)

Watercolor paint works nicely to add color details after your flowers are hardened.

INSTRUCTIONS

1. **Cut Petals**

   Trace petals from your templates onto the thin fabric and cut them out. Experiment with various shapes and sizes to achieve the desired look.

2. **Prepare Wire Stems**

   Using the wire cutters, cut the floral wire to a length of your choosing, allowing extra length to wrap and secure the fabric later.

3. **Melt Wax**

   Melt one pound of wax at a time, either in a double boiler or in a microwave, cooking on high in bursts of 15 to 20 seconds and stirring after each heating interval until the wax achieves a smooth and fully liquid state, at which point it is ready for use. Be cautious not to overheat or scorch, which may affect the fabric.

4. **Coat Fabric in Wax**

   Dip each fabric petal into the melted wax using a tool or your fingers, and spread the wax evenly on both sides with a small paintbrush. Coating the fabric in wax stiffens the petals, providing a more natural look and feel.

5. **Shape Petals**

   While the wax is still pliable, shape the petals to mimic the desired flower form. Gently fold or bend the waxed fabric to achieve realistic contours. Allow the petals to cool and harden.

6. **Create Center**

   Form a cluster using floral stamens or twist fine wires to create a central element. Using your paintbrush, secure this cluster with a small amount of melted wax.

7. **Attach Petals to Stems**

   Attach the waxed petals to the wire stems using your paintbrush and additional melted wax. Begin from the center and layer the petals outward, securing each layer with wax to create a cohesive structure.

8. **Add Layers and Details**

   Experiment with layering petals to achieve a fuller and more intricate appearance. Use melted wax to add subtle details and textures to the petals, mimicking the details on natural flowers.

9. **Final Touches**

   Allow the wax to cool and harden fully. Trim the stem to your preferred length, and refine any remaining details. The hardened wax provides stability to the flower structure.

10. **Optional Enhancements**

    If you're so inspired, lightly paint the dried waxed petals with watercolors to introduce subtle color variations and enhance the realism of the faux flowers.

JANE'S GARDENS

Jane's surviving letters, now cherished for the insights they provide into her daily life, family interactions, and literary musings, often touch upon her surroundings, including flowers. These letters, exploring family matters, social engagements, and literary discussions, subtly reveal glimpses into the gardens of and around her various homes in Steventon, Bath, Southampton, and Chawton, as well as the gardens and blooms she encountered in her travels.

In descriptions of Steventon, Jane vividly describes the blossoming beauty of the garden, reflecting on the abundance of nature around her. This window into the natural environment at Steventon offers insight into Jane's appreciation for the aesthetic pleasures of the rural setting of her childhood home. Primroses, anemones, and hyacinths, with their diverse colors, may have adorned the space alongside a traditional kitchen garden and orchard.

Bath, a city known for its Georgian architecture rather than its nature, may not have offered the sprawling grounds of Steventon, but the Austens' townhouse would likely have had a small garden. Jane was also known to frequent the Sydney Gardens, with its well-maintained flower-beds and gravel paths, which she described to Cassandra in her letters. Sydney Gardens often hosted large parties that included "... [concerts], with illuminations and fireworks." Jane, it seems, kept her distance from the excitement. She wrote to Cassandra in 1811: "... even the concert will have more than its usual charm for me, as the gardens are large enough for me to get pretty well beyond the reach of its sound."

In Southampton, where Jane lived for a short period, references to flowers in her letters provide insight into the local flora and the gardens surrounding her residence. The maritime influence of Southampton might have introduced her to coastal blooms, and her observations could have included the intertwining scents of sea air and garden blossoms. In their garden, the Austen women tended an array of colors with lilac, laburnum, and roses.

Later, when the women settled in Chawton, references to flowers, including sweet peas, violets, and roses, are scattered throughout Jane's correspondence. Chawton, with its more rural setting compared to Bath, provided her with a closer connection to the natural world. Here, she enjoyed a larger garden space near her home as well as a clear view of plentiful wildflowers in the countryside.

In these instances, the flowers in Jane's letters serve not only as an ode to nature but also as a testament to the changing landscapes of her life, which emerge in her novels.

During the Regency period, lavender water was a versatile cosmetic and fragrance. It was frequently used as a personal scent applied to the skin or clothing, offering a light and refreshing alternative to heavier perfumes. Additionally, lavender water was incorporated into toiletry routines, acting as a final touch after bathing to leave a subtle lavender aroma. Its use extended to freshening linens, clothes, and closets. The natural astringency of lavender made it suitable as a facial toner, believed to tighten and refresh the skin. In this era of elaborate hairstyles and wigs, lavender water became a fragrant mist, perfect for adding a touch of elegance to one's coiffure—and for hiding any odors emanating from unwashed wigs.

Beyond its cosmetic applications, lavender water was associated with relaxation and good health. It was often used as a calming mist in the bedroom or sprayed on pillows to aid in restful sleep. Some believed a lavender-soaked compress could relieve a headache. Lavender's pleasant scent and antibacterial properties made it a natural deodorant, and its mild disinfectant qualities were useful when applied to minor cuts and abrasions, promoting healing and preventing infection.

This simple lavender water recipe captures the essence of a natural cosmetic and medicinal product from the Regency era:

YIELD: 8 OUNCES OF LAVENDER WATER

INGREDIENTS AND MATERIALS

Glass Jar (8 ounces)
A glass jar with a tight-fitting lid is essential for storing the product during the infusion process. Glass is nonreactive and helps maintain the potency of the ingredients.

Fresh or Dried Lavender (4 tablespoons fresh or 2 tablespoons dried)
Lavender adds a pleasant, soothing fragrance to the water. Fresh lavender can be harvested from your garden or purchased from a local flower market, while dried organic lavender can be found at specialty stores or online. It's essential to ensure that your lavender hasn't been sprayed with harmful pesticides or chemicals—especially if you plan to use it on your body or clothing.

Distilled Water (1 cup)
Distilled water is free from impurities and minerals, making it ideal for skincare. It serves as the base of the product, providing hydration without the risk of contamination.

Vodka or Witch Hazel (2 tablespoons)
Vodka or witch hazel acts as a natural preservative, extending the product's shelf life by inhibiting bacterial growth. Vodka has antimicrobial properties, while witch hazel is a natural astringent known for its skin-soothing benefits.

Cheesecloth or Fine Strainer
Cheesecloth or a fine strainer is necessary for filtering out the lavender buds from the infused product.

Dark Glass Bottle or Jar (8 ounces)
For storing the product after it has been infused. Dark glass bottles are ideal for protecting the contents from the degrading effects of light exposure.

INSTRUCTIONS

1. **Clean Jar**

   Just as you would sanitize a jar before using it to can food, sterilize your glass jar by boiling it for five minutes. Let the jar cool and dry before moving to the next step!

2. **Add Lavender**

   Scoop your fresh or dried lavender flowers into the glass jar.

3. **Add Distilled Water**

   Pour your distilled water into the jar, covering the lavender completely.

4. **Add Preservative**

   Add vodka or witch hazel to the jar to prevent the growth of bacteria and preserve the lavender water.

5. **Seal Jar**

   Tightly seal the jar with the lid. Ensure it is closed securely to prevent evaporation or leakage.

6. **Infuse**

   Place the jar in a cool, dark place for two weeks to allow the lavender to infuse into the water. Shake the jar gently every few days to help the process along.

7. **Strain**

   After two weeks, strain the lavender water using cheesecloth or a fine strainer to remove the lavender flowers. This process will leave you with a clear lavender-infused liquid that's ready to be used.

8. **Store in Dark Glass Bottle or Jar**

   Pour the strained lavender water into a clean, dry, dark bottle. Store in the refrigerator for up to one month, or freeze for up to one year.

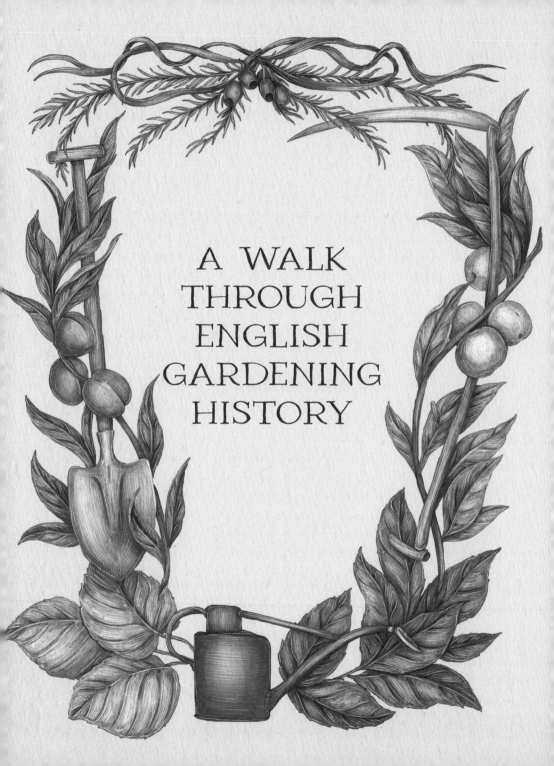

A WALK
THROUGH
ENGLISH
GARDENING
HISTORY

he quintessence of English landscape design has long embraced structured informality, the planning of a garden to intentionally convey the appearance of spontaneity. Despite trends shifting over the years, the enduring hallmark of the English garden remains best described as "designed chaos." Even in contemporary times, the English garden continues to rely on meticulously arranged, visually appealing elements strategically positioned and cultivated to create the illusion of a wild and natural space. But has this stylistic orientation persisted throughout history? Certainly not.

The Romans introduced their signature garden designs to Britannia, leaving a lasting impact on the landscape with planned social spaces seen in surviving Roman ruins. Adapting to the wetter English climate, they created an array of gardens during their occupation from AD 43 to the early fifth century, from private gardens to public recreational spaces.

Later, practicality governed the cultivation of crops and medicinal plants during the Middle Ages. Monasteries played a central role in food and medicine production, serving communities as mandated by the monarchy. Enclosed monastery gardens were used to grow functional, utilitarian crops and herbs. They were also havens for meditation and recreation.

Tudor gardens, influenced by Italian Renaissance designs, were meticulously crafted to captivate observers. These formal landscapes comprised high-walled spaces that housed various gardens, including knot gardens, kitchen gardens, mazes, and fishponds. Building upon the medieval foundations, Tudor gardens offered surprises at every turn, with strategically placed seating providing captivating views. The sixteenth and seventeenth centuries saw the creative contributions of the Tradescant men: John the elder and John the younger.

Collaborating with influential figures, they integrated plants discovered during colonial exploration into English gardens, sparking advancements in design.

As the Tudor era ended, larger manor houses and estates embraced expansive formal landscape designs spanning their entire grounds. Influenced by prominent landscape designers in Holland and France, these designs often featured vast, formal landscapes with grand, flat terraces known as parterres. These parterres evolved from existing Tudor knot gardens. Stuart-era gardens showcased long avenues of trees, artificial hills called view mounts, statues, and water. This style also highlighted sculpted shrubs as well as foreign bulbs and perennials. Mastery over nature was the name of the game, with gardeners manipulating the landscape.

English society underwent a transformative shift in the early eighteenth century, particularly in gardens and landscaping. Previously influenced by French ideals of rigid order and formal symmetry, a new trend emerged known as the "landscape style." This movement emphasized naturalistic landscapes and vistas, rejecting the artificial form and control of French designs. The mid-eighteenth century saw the widespread influence of Lancelot "Capability" Brown, renowned for his pastoral designs crafted for affluent estates such as Stowe and Chatsworth. Brown's work left a lasting impact, influencing numerous landscape designs across England, including those at Highclere Castle and Blenheim Palace, which remain well-known examples today.

Following Capability Brown's death in 1783, Humphry Repton, another prominent English landscape designer and a peer of Brown's, emerged as the new proponent of the landscape style. Repton promoted the inclusion of decorative objects, like containers and buildings, in his designs, emphasizing the concept of "eye-catchers" to conceal hidden treasures. Under Repton, the naturalistic trend evolved into an obsession with the untamed, giving rise to a dramatic style characterized by artificial ruins and expansive wilderness areas. Ironically, these so-called "wild" landscapes required careful tending by gardeners. In the Regency era, significant alterations to the landscape were commonplace, including tree relocation, hill creation or leveling, pond construction, and river rerouting, all of which were intended to give the landscape the look of a perfectly framed picture.

THE NOVELS

Take a moment to rediscover Jane Austen's novels:

SENSE AND SENSIBILITY (1811)

Set against the backdrop of late-1700s South West England, *Sense and Sensibility* shares the tale of the Dashwood sisters—Elinor, Marianne, and Margaret—whose lives take an unexpected turn after their father's untimely death forces them to leave their cherished home estate, Norland Park. Resignedly, they embrace the offer of a humbler abode, Barton Cottage, from a relative. As they adjust to their new environment, Elinor and Marianne—with the younger Margaret tagging along—embark on a journey through life. They encounter the highs of love and the lows of heartbreak and one very reserved, handsome Colonel Brandon.

PRIDE AND PREJUDICE (1813)

In *Pride and Prejudice,* Mr. Bennet is the proud owner of the Longbourn estate, sharing his residence with his wife and their five daughters, including the beloved Elizabeth Bennet. As Elizabeth navigates a complex social landscape, she encounters the enigmatic Mr. Darcy, leading to a tumultuous relationship marked by (as the title suggests!) pride and prejudice. The novel explores the intricacies of manners, morality, and the pursuit of personal happiness in a society in which social standing and financial considerations play a significant role in romantic relationships.

MANSFIELD PARK (1814)

Mansfield Park chronicles the life of Fanny Price, a character who stands out as one of Jane Austen's most complex and controversial heroines. Unlike Austen's typical protagonists, Fanny hails from a lower social class and is a timid, sensitive girl who shies away from attention. The novel follows Fanny's journey from childhood to adulthood, hinging on her relocation, at age ten, to her aunt and uncle's estate, Mansfield Park. There, she encounters an intricate web of relationships, including her cousin Edmund's tumultuous romance with a woman who disapproves of his clerical aspirations. The sprawling rural estate serves as the backdrop for the novel's exploration of character, morality, and social hierarchy.

EMMA (1815)

Emma, Jane's fourth novel, is set in fictional High-bury, England, and its surrounding country estates. The story revolves around Emma Woodhouse, a precocious, privileged young woman who misuses her confidence and intelligence by playing match-maker. Her comical obsession with meddling in her friends' romantic lives often leads her to neglect her own emotions and overlook potential relationships, specifically one with her dear friend George Knightley. This endearing flaw creates a delightful dichotomy for the reader and is surely a reason why Emma remains one of Austen's most beloved and relatable characters.

NORTHANGER ABBEY (1817)

Northanger Abbey, Jane Austen's clever satire of the gothic novel, tells the story of Catherine Morland, a young and impres-sionable seventeen-year-old. With a blend of naivete and curiosity, Catherine embarks on her first journey into the world without her family, where she grapples with the intricacies of high society and the unfamiliar landscape of Bath. She meets Henry Tilney, a charming clergyman and son of a local landowner, who initially seems indifferent to her affections. As the narrative unfolds, it becomes apparent that Catherine's fascination with gothic fiction and her reliance on socioeconomic stereo-types distort her perceptions of those around her, including the endearing Tilney, leading to a jour-ney of self-discovery and growth.

PERSUASION (1817)

Persuasion follows Anne Elliot, a 27-year-old woman who, by Regency standards, is considered beyond her prime. Her father, Sir Walter Elliot, faces financial troubles and is forced to rent out their family home to Admiral Croft and his wife. Unbeknownst to Anne, the admiral's brother, Captain Frederick Wentworth, is a former love interest to whom she was engaged seven years prior. When Captain Wentworth returns, their reunion sparks a series of awkward and romantic encounters, leading to a journey of self-discovery and second chances.

Rose

ROSA SPP.

Roses can be upright, climbing, or trailing shrubs, depending on the variety. The stem of the rose is typically covered with thorns of assorted sizes and shapes, although there are varieties with few to no thorns at all.

Throughout the growing season, the rose produces waves of flowers. The number of petals will differ depending on whether the rose is wild or a bred cultivar. A wild rose typically has one layer of five petals, while cultivated roses usually have double—and sometimes triple—the layers of petals. During the Georgian and the Regency periods in

England, fewer than two hundred varieties of roses belonging to the *Rosa* genus existed. These roses are now classified as "old-world" roses.

NORTHANGER ABBEY

In the first chapter of *Northanger Abbey*, Jane describes Catherine Morland as the sort of child who preferred roughhousing with the boys to tending a garden:

> *A family of ten children will be always called a fine family, where there are heads and arms and legs enough for the number; but the Morlands had little other right to the word, for they were in general very plain, and Catherine, for many years of her life, as plain as any. She had a thin awkward figure, a sallow skin without color, dark lank hair, and strong features—so much for her person; and not less unpropitious for heroism seemed her mind. She was fond of all boys' plays, and greatly preferred cricket not merely to dolls, but to the more heroic enjoyments of infancy, nursing a dormouse, feeding a canary-bird, or watering a **rose-bush**. Indeed she had no taste for a garden; and if she gathered flowers at all, it was chiefly for the pleasure of mischief—at least so it was conjectured from her always preferring those which she was forbidden to take. Such were her propensities—her abilities were quite as extraordinary.*

MANSFIELD PARK

In *Mansfield Park*, the Bertrams and Mrs. Norris scold Fanny for spending too much time outside in the heat of the day. Fanny had lingered in the garden, cutting and tending to the roses:

> *"I was out above an hour. I sat three-quarters of an hour in the flower-garden, while Fanny cut the **roses**; and very pleasant it was, I assure you, but very hot. It was shady enough in the alcove, but I declare I quite dreaded the coming home again."*
>
> *"Fanny has been cutting **roses**, has she?"*

"Yes, and I am afraid they will be the last this year. Poor thing! She found it hot enough; but they were so full-blown that one could not wait." . . .

"But were there **roses** *enough to oblige her to go twice?"*

"No; but they were to be put into the spare room to dry; and, unluckily, Fanny forgot to lock the door of the room and bring away the key, so she was obliged to go again."

JANE AUSTEN, HER LIFE AND LETTERS: A FAMILY RECORD

In February 1807, Jane Austen penned a letter to Cassandra from Southampton, enthusiastically sharing updates about the progress of the garden and walkways at her home, and showcasing her love for nature and her joy in observing its beauty:

Our garden is putting in order by a man who bears a remarkably good character, has a very fine complexion, and asks something less than the first. The shrubs which border the gravel walk, he says, are only sweetbriar and **roses***, and the latter of an indifferent sort; we mean to get a few of the better kind, therefore, and at my own particular desire he procures us some syringas. I could not do without a syringa, for the sake of Cowper's line. We talk also of a laburnum. The border under the terrace wall is clearing away to receive currants and gooseberry bushes, and a spot is found very proper for raspberries.*

A SHORT HISTORY OF ROSES

The rose has left its botanical footprint across the Northern Hemisphere through fossil evidence dating back an impressive thirty-five million years. While the wild boasts an impressive variety of approximately 150 rose species, cultivation of these elegant flowers traces its roots to ancient China, where the practice is believed to have begun around five thousand years ago.

The dissemination of roses across continents owes much to the bustling trade routes of the Silk Road, which facilitated their journey from the Far East to Europe. Along the way were the Romans, who played a pivotal role in introducing roses to England and the rest of Europe. By the fifteenth century, roses had transcended their origins to become potent symbols in English society, notably embodying the rival royal houses of York and Lancaster, whose bitter feud is immortalized in history as the Wars of the Roses. By the time the Regency era began, English gardeners had at least 150 rose varieties to choose from, each boasting a stunning palette ranging from pristine white to vibrant purple. Among the beloved old-world roses were the damask, centifolia, moss, alba, and gallica, which adorned gardens with their timeless charm. Whether planted in dedicated formal gardens or nestled in large pots for easy transport between terraces or winter sheltering in hothouses, roses held a key place in Regency landscapes.

Today, roses continue to captivate gardeners all over the world while maintaining their status as an enduring symbol of beauty and elegance. Through meticulous breeding efforts, modern roses blend the charm of old-world varieties with improved attributes like extended bloom times, disease resistance, and a rich diversity of shapes, sizes, and colors.

REGENCY ROSES

During the Regency era, roses were a staple in English gardens, symbolizing purity, virtue, and romance. Here are some of the most popular types of roses during that time:

ALBA

Alba roses, one of the oldest varieties, were likely introduced to England by the Romans. They are recognized for their blue-green foliage and semi-double to double flowers in shades ranging from pure white to blush pink. They typically bloom once in early summer and are highly fragrant, emitting a sweet, delicate scent.

During the Renaissance, alba roses became a common feature in English gardens, symbolizing purity and virtue among the nobility. Throughout the Tudor years, they symbolized the Virgin Mary in religious iconography. The seventeenth and eighteenth centuries witnessed an increased interest in botany, leading gardeners to cultivate and hybridize albas, resulting in new varieties with enhanced fragrance and larger blooms.

The Regency era solidified the place of alba roses in English horticulture. With their delicate blooms and robust nature, alba roses became essential in garden designs. Their sprawling growth habit allowed the rose to fit perfectly into romantic, pastoral landscapes. Albas were also commonly used in bouquets, posies, and other floral arrangements for their strong scent and long vase life.

BOURBON

The bourbon rose is famous for its abundant blooms, which come in a variety of colors, from soft pastels to rich, deep hues. These roses bloom repeatedly throughout the season, creating a continuous display of color and fragrance in the garden.

Introduced to English gardens in the early nineteenth century by French botanists and rose enthusiasts, bourbon roses are a result of crossing different varieties, specifically the damask and the China rose. During the Regency era, new rose varieties from France frequently found their way into the gardens of English socialites. Throughout the nineteenth century, bourbon roses were a popular choice for landscapes and gardens all over England, appreciated for their showy blooms.

CENTIFOLIA

The centifolia rose, also known as the Holland or Provence rose, has a rich history that dates back to Holland in the sixteenth century before quickly reaching English gardens. A cross between alba and damask roses, the centifolia rose blooms just once during the growing season, but its magnificent display is worth the wait. With its large, luxuriant blooms boasting upwards of a hundred petals, it has earned the nickname "cabbage rose."

During the Regency era, this rose found favor among the fashionable elite, adorning the landscapes of grand estates and country manors across the English countryside. From the bustling streets of London to the tranquil gardens of rural retreats, the centifolia could be found in all corners of the country. The centifolia rose sparked inspiration in poets, artists, and garden enthusiasts of the time, eliciting odes and sonnets that praised its loveliness. Its timeless charm and classic allure made it a symbol of romance and passion, with its blossoms adorning bridal bouquets and garden trellises as a testament to its enduring appeal.

CHINA

The China rose, heralded for its exotic allure and vibrant blooms, first appeared in English gardens in the late eighteenth century, when it was introduced from its native China. Also known as the Bengal rose, the plant is renowned for its prolific blooming habit. The China rose bears clusters of flowers in a kaleidoscope of hues, ranging from delicate pinks to fiery reds and rich purples. Its distinctive blooms, often marked by a prominent yellow center, give off a sweet, spicy fragrance.

During the Regency era, the China rose was widely popular. Its vibrant blooms added a unique splash of color to formal rose gardens and informal borders. The rose provided an array of bloom colors that weren't typically seen in other roses of the time, which made them highly valued and sought after.

DAMASK

The damask rose has a rich history in England with two potential origin stories. One story credits Crusader Robert de Brie with introducing the rose to Europe in the eleventh century, from where it eventually made its way to England. Another legend suggests that Henry VIII received the rose in the sixteenth century. Regardless of how it arrived in England, the rose flourished and became a staple of English horticulture.

Characterized by their lush, full blooms, damask roses have velvet petals in hues of pink, crimson, or white. They were a common sight in Regency gardens, where they were often placed strategically to create informal borders. The damask rose also held a special place in Regency culture, being used in perfumes, potpourris, and culinary dishes.

MOSS

With its mossy-looking stems and delicate flowers, the moss rose became prevalent in English gardens during the Regency era after being introduced in the eighteenth century. Its unique appearance made it stand out, while its gentle fragrance, reminiscent of pine trees in the forest, added to its appeal. The plant has glands on its sepals that secrete resin, which gives off a distinct scent when disturbed. The moss rose thrived in both formal beds and in containers and was commonly placed in areas with high foot traffic so they could be brushed against, releasing fragrance into the garden.

NOISETTE

The Noisette rose was developed in the early nineteenth century and became popular in English gardens during the Regency era. It was named after the French nurseryman Philippe Noisette's nursery in Charleston, South Carolina. With its clusters of fragrant blooms in shades of soft pink, creamy white, and pale yellow, this rose variety quickly gained favor after being brought back to Europe. In English gardens, the Noisette rose was often seen trailing up arbors, trellises, and pergolas due to its long canes and rapid growth habit, making it an ideal climbing rose. The blooms also had a long vase life, making them perfect for posies, bouquets, and floral arrangements.

FROM HER PEN TO THE PETAL: AUSTEN-INSPIRED ROSES

It's no surprise that roses have become synonymous with Jane Austen's work, as they embody the romance and elegance of the Regency era. In recent years, rose breeders have created stunning varieties to celebrate Austen-related anniversaries and milestones. Here are just a few that are still available on the market today:

PRIDE AND PREJUDICE ROSE® (2013)

Renowned English rose breeder Harkness Rose Company introduced the Pride and Prejudice rose to commemorate the novel's 200th anniversary. This beauty blooms in shades of blush pink and cream and has a sweet, soft fragrance.

JANE AUSTEN ROSE® (2017)

Harkness Rose Company also revealed the Jane Austen rose to mark the 200th anniversary of Jane's passing. This unique rose boasts rich, deep-orange petals, deviating from the typical soft shades associated with Austen and the Regency era.

PRIDE OF JANE COLLECTION (2017–2018)

Breeder Jan Spek Rozen introduced the Pride of Jane collection, featuring six exquisite roses:

Bloomsbury®
This rose is a pale soft pink with a delicate fragrance.

Emma Woodhouse®
This rose is a dusky light-peach color with a delicate fragrance and large blooms.

Hydepark®
The Hydepark® rose is a creamy yellow with a soft, distinct fragrance.

Lady Carolina®

This rose is a vibrant coral-pink variety with a strong, fruity fragrance.

Mansfield Park®

The Mansfield Park rose is a soft blush-pink variety with a light, sweet fragrance. Its blooms are full and lush.

Pride of Jane®

This rose is a delicate pink variety with a moderate, sweet fragrance.

CULTIVATING JANE

Design a Posy Bouquet

In the Regency era, posy bouquets held a significance that transcended their beauty, reflecting the societal values and modes of expression of the time. These delicate handheld floral arrangements served multiple purposes, extending beyond mere ornamentation to convey symbolic meanings and fulfill practical functions in daily life. Their charm and significance were deeply woven into the fabric of everyday existence, making them an integral part of the era's cultural landscape.

Posies became powerful messengers, conveying sentiments and emotions that often couldn't be relayed with just words. These petite bouquets allowed individuals to express sentiments discreetly or make subtle statements through the language of flowers. Whether exchanged between lovers as secret tokens of affection or presented during social engagements to convey well-wishes, posies became a nuanced form of communication in an era when societal conventions often dictated restraint.

Posy bouquets also served a practical purpose. In a time when personal hygiene was not as advanced as today, the sweet-smelling herbs within posies were strategically chosen not only for their symbolic significance but also for their ability to mask less pleasant odors. Carrying a posy became a fashionable and practical accessory, providing a delightful fragrance that accompanied individuals throughout their day.

Today, posy bouquets have retained their versatility. While no longer laden with the same societal codes, these charming arrangements, with their timeless beauty, still find a place in our lives, gracing weddings, celebrations, and everyday moments. Understanding posies' historical richness and practical utility reminds us that the language of flowers and the art of bouquet crafting have enduring roots.

YIELD: 1 SMALL HANDHELD POSY BOUQUET

MATERIALS

Fresh Flowers (3 to 5 stems)

Choose a variety of fresh flowers in colors and shapes that appeal to you, such as roses, violets, lavender, and forget-me-nots. Each type of flower will contribute its unique beauty and fragrance to the posy.

Fragrant Herbs (3 to 5 stems)

Fragrant herbs, like rosemary and mint, add an aromatic element to your posy. Rosemary and mint are practical choices for their pleasant scents and attractive foliage.

Small, Lightweight Greenery (3 to 4 stems)

Greenery adds texture and volume to the posy, enhancing its visual appeal. Look for delicate foliage, such as fern or boxwood, to complement the flowers without overpowering them.

Garden Shears

You will need scissors or garden shears to trim the stems of the flowers and greenery to the desired length. Sharp, clean cuts ensure the longevity of your posy and facilitate easy arranging.

Ribbon or Twine (1 to 2 yards)

Ribbon or twine serves as a decorative accent and helps bind the posy together. Choose your adornments in colors that pair well and match the overall theme.

INSTRUCTIONS

1. **Select Flowers**

   Consider choosing flowers that were commonly used during the Regency era, focusing on those with delicate and pastel-colored blooms. Roses, violets, lavender, and forget-me-nots were favorites! Include flowers with symbolic meanings if that's something you enjoy. For example, honeysuckle would signal that you have devoted affection for someone, an iris that you are a loyal friend, or a white rose might indicate innocence and purity.

2. **Select Herbs**

   Pick fragrant herbs, like rosemary or mint, to complement the flowers and add a delightful scent.

3. **Add Greenery**

   Include small and lightweight greenery to add texture and balance to the bouquet. Consider what foliage, like ferns or boxwood, would best complement the chosen flowers and herbs.

4. **Trim Stems**

   Trim the stems of your selected flowers, herbs, and greenery to a length of about 6 inches. They should be long enough for a comfortable grip but short enough to maintain the compact size of the posy.

5. **Arrange Posy**

   Start by holding a central flower or herb in your hand and gradually add others around it, creating a rounded and compact shape. Balance a mix of colors and textures as you build the bouquet. The posy should be small enough to be held in one hand.

6. **Secure with Ribbon or Twine**

   Once you are satisfied with the arrangement, tie the stems together using a ribbon or twine.

7. **Tidy Stems**

   Examine the stems to ensure they are trimmed to a uniform length, which will give the posy a neat and polished appearance. Further trim any outliers.

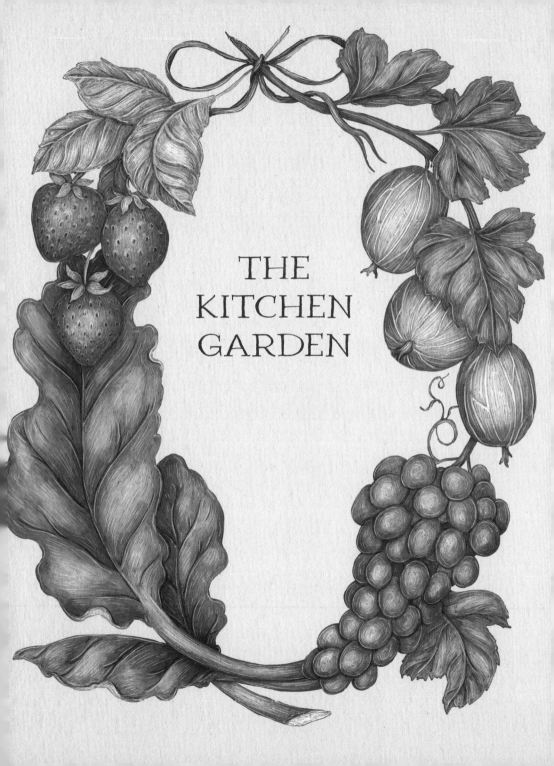

THE
KITCHEN
GARDEN

uring the Regency era, kitchen gardens were integral to households, providing fresh produce and culinary herbs. These gardens were not exclusive to a specific type of house; instead, they were found in a range of residences, each reflecting the social and economic standing of the occupants.

Kitchen gardens during this time were meticulously planned spaces designed to meet the culinary and medicinal needs of the household. The layout often featured geometric designs with rectangular or square plots separated by well-defined paths. While larger estates prominently displayed expansive gardens, smaller urban residences and cottages embraced the practice more modestly.

In grand country estates, the kitchen garden was a fundamental component of the household, signaling the wealth and status of the landowner. These estates had the space and resources to maintain extensive kitchen gardens to grow a wide variety of vegetables, herbs, and medicinal plants. The gardens were often adjacent to the house, emphasizing the convenience of access and the symbiotic relationship between the kitchen and the garden.

Country houses of varying sizes, from the opulent manors of the aristocracy to more modest rural dwellings, incorporated kitchen gardens into their landscapes. These homes recognized the practicality and economic advantages of growing their own produce, aligning with the period's emphasis on self-sufficiency. In townhouses and urban residences, where space was limited, kitchen gardens or herb gardens were adapted to fit the constraints of city living. These plots were practical and efficient, focusing on essential herbs and select vegetables. Cottages and rural homes commonly maintained kitchen gardens, albeit on a smaller scale than their grander counterparts. These gardens reflected the practical needs of the household, supplying fresh produce for daily meals. Despite the size differences, the design principles remained similar, featuring geometric layouts and well-organized beds.

CULTIVATING JANE

Create a Container Kitchen Garden

Re-creating a Regency-style kitchen garden is not merely a horticultural endeavor; it is a step back in time, inviting the charm and elegance of the early nineteenth century into your backyard. This project is an ode to the culinary and botanical traditions of Jane Austen's era, when kitchen gardens provided sustenance for the household and a symphony of fragrances and colors.

As you dive in, envision containers brimming with heirloom vegetables, culinary herbs, and medicinal plants that once adorned the landscapes of grand estates and modest cottages. Planning carefully is essential, as it will allow you to create a contained kitchen garden that is both beautiful and useful for your own household needs.

WHAT WILL YOU PLANT?

There are many plants to consider for your kitchen garden. Here are just a few you might like to grow:

Culinary Herbs
Rosemary, thyme, basil, lemon balm, parsley, sage, marjoram

Vegetables
Heirloom tomatoes, traditional carrot varieties, peas, beans, cabbage

Medicinal Plants
Chamomile, lavender, calendula, mint

Fruits
Apples, strawberries, currants

Some plants aren't only ornamental; they can also be useful. For instance:

- **Marigolds** deter pests.
- **Nasturtiums** have edible petals and leaves that add a peppery kick to salads.
- **Chives** not only taste good but they also disguise the scent of carrots growing in the garden to help keep the pests away.

Note: Remember to check your local climate and soil conditions to ensure the optimal growth of these plants. Also, if you have a garden plot, all of these can be planted directly in the ground!

MATERIALS

Journal or Notebook
This will help you to organize, plan, and document your progress.

Garden Container(s)
Determine the space you have available for your kitchen garden. If space is limited, use small containers, such as pots and window boxes. If you have more room, consider using a 20 by 40-inch rectangular planter, which will give you plenty of space to grow an assortment of edibles. Make sure your container has drainage holes!

Potting Mix (2 cubic feet)
Choose a high-quality potting mix. The soil should be loose, well draining, and rich in organic matter to support healthy plant growth.

Seedlings (8 to 10)
Select a variety of herbs, vegetables, and fruits you enjoy cooking with. Consider heirloom varieties and plants with culinary and medicinal uses, especially those that were common during the Regency era, such as strawberries, thyme, and peppermint. You may also want to incorporate companion-planting techniques. For example, plant basil near tomatoes to improve their flavor and to deter pests. You can purchase seedlings

from a nursery or garden center, or, if you're ambitious, try to start your vegetable seeds indoors before planting time!

Trellis or Wooden Support (optional)

A trellis or wooden support can be used as a decorative element or to provide extra stability for growing plants. We often think of trellises as a wide lattice framework, but they come in all shapes, configurations, and sizes, and can fit in a variety of containers.

Plant Tags

Use these to keep track of the plant names and varieties, lest you forget!

Watering Can or Hose

Ensure you have a reliable method for regularly watering your kitchen garden. A watering can or hose with a gentle spray nozzle is ideal for giving plants the moisture they need to thrive.

Vegetable Fertilizer (1-pound bag)

Depending on your plants' nutrient needs, you may have to fertilize your kitchen garden periodically. Choose a balanced fertilizer suitable for vegetables and herbs, and follow the manufacturer's instructions for application. If you can, adhere to organic gardening practices, as many modern chemical pesticides and fertilizers were not commonly used during the Regency era.

Garden Gloves

Gloves will help protect your skin and nails while you plant and harvest.

INSTRUCTIONS

1. **Research and Plan**

   In the spring, begin your journey by choosing plants, vegetables, and herbs that will work for your space. Make a list in your journal. Select a sunny spot for your kitchen garden container, ensuring it will get 6 to 8 hours of sunlight each day.

2. **Plant Seedlings**

Fill your container(s) with the potting mix, leaving an inch or two at the top to make watering easier. Dig a hole large enough for the seedling's root ball. Then, gently work the seedling out of its current pot and place it in the hole. Fill around the roots with potting mix, making sure none are visible. Gently pat the soil around the base of the plant. Be careful not to overcrowd your plants! In general, follow these spacing guidelines:

Cucumbers and squash: 12 inches

Herbs: 6 inches

Fruiting vegetables: 12 inches

Leafy greens: 5 inches

Root vegetables: 3 inches

After planting all your seedlings, water thoroughly.

3. **Add Supports and Plant Tags**

Consider incorporating a trellis or wooden support for climbing plants, like peas and pole beans. These structures serve a practical purpose and add a decorative element to your garden. Wooden and ceramic plant markers are also attractive and helpful for organization.

4. **Maintenance**

Tend to your container garden by weeding, watering, fertilizing, and harvesting regularly. Remember to wear gardening gloves!

5. **Document Progress**

Use your journal to record your gardening activities, including details such as planting schedules, weather conditions, and growth observations. This will help you track harvest times and plan for future seasons—an essential practice in the Regency kitchen garden.

JANE'S KITCHEN GARDENS

Jane lived in a world where kitchen gardens were a mainstay. Her early years at Steventon Rectory in Hampshire would have included a typical kitchen garden, a hallmark of rural parsonages during the late eighteenth century. Vegetables, herbs, and fruit trees would have thrived, catering to the culinary needs of the Austen household.

The family's move to Bath marked a shift from Steventon's rustic charm to the Georgian city's sophisticated allure. Bath, known for its architectural grandeur, wasn't the ideal place for expansive gardens. Yet, even within the urban landscape, the Austens likely had access to a small kitchen garden.

After a brief stay in Southampton, the Austen family settled permanently in Chawton. This quaint village in Hampshire became the backdrop for the latter part of Jane's life and her prolific literary output. The cottage in Chawton, now the Jane Austen's House museum, stands as a tangible link to the horticultural domesticity defining those years. The museum has re-created the home's gardens, including the kitchen garden that would have been an integral part of the Austen home.

Cabbage

BRASSICA OLERACEA VAR. CAPITATA

Cabbage is a vegetable plant that is part of the mustard family, which includes kale, broccoli, brussels sprouts, and head cabbage. However, when most people use the word "cabbage," they are referring to the head cabbage.

EMMA

Cabbage beds are mentioned in *Emma* as Mrs. Elton and Mr. Knightley converge to create alternate plans for a group exploring trip and picnic after a carriage horse turns up lame. Mr. Knightley tempts Mrs. Elton with the promise of strawberries at an alternative location, but Jane explains via the narration that Mrs. Elton could have been enticed by something as plain as cabbages, as she simply wanted to go somewhere and do something:

*If Mr. Knightley did not begin seriously, he was obliged to proceed so, for his proposal was caught at with delight; and the "Oh! I should like it of all things," was not plainer in words than manner. Donwell was famous for its strawberry-beds, which seemed a plea for the invitation: but no plea was necessary; **cabbage**-beds would have been enough to tempt the lady, who only wanted to be going somewhere. She promised him again and again to come—much oftener than he doubted—and was extremely gratified by such a proof of intimacy, such a distinguishing compliment as she chose to consider it.*

A SHORT HISTORY OF CABBAGE

Various forms of agricultural cabbage have grown naturally around the world for thousands of years and have been a part of many diets in England for centuries. The climate in England ensured that cabbage could be a year-round crop. Both abundant and affordable, cabbage was used in main courses, soups and salads, and sometimes as decoration. During the Regency era, cabbage grew in almost every kitchen garden, often with an entire section to itself. It wasn't uncommon for many head gardeners to create patterns and designs using different varieties of cabbage with unique colors and textures.

Today, cabbages remain one of the most widely cultivated and consumed vegetables across the globe. They are appreciated for their versatility, nutritional value, and broad culinary appeal. More than seventy-two million tons of cabbage and other brassica are produced around the world per year and are consumed in a variety of ways: steamed, boiled, pickled, baked, fried, and raw.

Currants

RIBES RUBRUM OR *RIBES NIGRUM*

COMMON NAMES: RED CURRANTS, BLACK CURRANTS, CASSIS

The red **currant**, or *Ribes rubrum,* a member of the gooseberry family, grows wild all over England. A hardy, deciduous shrub that can grow more than four feet tall at maturity, *R. rubrum* is easy to grow, tolerant of shade, and can be planted even in northern exposure. While other varieties of currants sometimes have spines, red currants have smooth branches. The shrub produces flowers in drooping clusters in the spring, and juicy red berries appear in early summer.

R. nigrum is very similar to the red currant, with only a few differences, mainly in the leaves and fruit. The leaves of the black currant are hairy and can have a very geometric shape. Black currant fruits are round, black berries.

EMMA

In *Emma,* currants are mentioned alongside strawberries when Mrs. Elton describes her berry-picking woes. Although she goes on at length about "strawberries, and only strawberries," Mrs. Elton concedes that "**currants** [are] more refreshing." (See page 55 for the complete excerpt.)

While it's possible that Jane was referencing any number of currant cultivars, more than likely, she meant the common red currant, *Ribes rubrum*, or the black currant, *Ribes nigrum.*

A SHORT HISTORY OF CURRANTS

The red currant is native to western Europe and naturalized in England. Black currants are non-native to England and originally came by way of Sweden and Norway. Red currants were first recorded in Britain in 1568, while black currants have grown in England since the seventeenth century. It's possible that *R. rubrum* is native to England, but because the terms "native" and "naturalized" are used interchangeably in some records, it's impossible to tell. During the Regency, currants were an essential source of nutrients and could be found in many sweet and savory recipes. They were also used to make wine and cordials.

Currants are now widely cultivated in England and the rest of the United Kingdom and Europe. They remain desired for their delicious fruits, which, while tart when eaten fresh, are extremely high in vitamin C. Raw black currants have a strong, bitter flavor and generally need to be cooked, but red currants have a juicy, tart-sweet taste even when eaten raw. Both varieties, properly prepared, make a tasty addition to jams, baked desserts, smoothies, and salads.

Potato

SOLANUM TUBEROSUM

COMMON NAMES: IRISH POTATO, WHITE POTATO

Potatoes, or *Solanum tuberosum,* are cool-weather perennial vegetables that produce vining foliage up to two feet long. After the plant flowers, forms fruit, and produces tubers, the foliage dies back, signaling that the potatoes are ready to be dug and harvested.

There are more than five thousand potato varieties, each producing a different tuber. There are seemingly infinite combinations of colors, tuber sizes, and consistencies. White, pink, yellow, and deep-purple tuber flesh can all be found.

MANSFIELD PARK

During a dinner, an argument descends on the table over the improvement of Sotherton Court. When debating the value and labor behind harvesting apricots, Dr. Grant compares the fruit of Mrs. Norris's cherished apricot tree to the bland flavor of a potato:

> *"You were imposed on, ma'am," replied Dr. Grant: "these **potatoes** have as much the flavour of a Moor Park apricot as the fruit from that tree. It is an insipid fruit at the best; but a good apricot is eatable, which none from my garden are."*

A SHORT HISTORY OF POTATOES

Originating in the Andes Mountains region of South America, the potato embarked on a transformative journey that would see it become a culinary staple in England and beyond. Sir Walter Raleigh is often credited with introducing this versatile vegetable to

England, bringing it back from Virginia in 1586. However, its initial reception was far from enthusiastic.

For centuries, potatoes were relegated to the status of food for the poor and fodder for livestock. It wasn't until the mid-1600s that the Royal Horticultural Society took the initiative to change this perception and promote the use of potatoes. With concerted efforts, potatoes gradually began to appear on tables across the country, shedding their stigma as a lowly foodstuff.

By the mid-1700s, potatoes had undergone a remarkable transformation, fully integrating into English cuisine. During the Regency era, they became a ubiquitous presence in numerous dishes and were cultivated extensively in gardens and larger farms, serving as a vital food crop for the nation.

Today, potatoes are some of the most readily available and versatile vegetables worldwide. Their appeal lies not only in their taste but also in their ability to be prepared in countless ways, from mashed and fried to baked and beyond. Beyond their culinary uses, potatoes have also found surprising applications, such as serving as natural cleaning agents for both leather and glass.

CULTIVATING JANE

Grow Potatoes in Grow Bags

Among the crops that can flourish in a kitchen garden, potatoes are an exceptionally gratifying one. Potatoes are versatile, delicious, and surprisingly easy to cultivate, making them an ideal addition to your gardening repertoire. Whether you're a seasoned gardener or a beginner with a green thumb, cultivating your own potatoes is an adventure that easily brings the joy of homegrown goodness to your table—even if you don't have garden space to grow them!

Potatoes are some of the easiest vegetables to grow in a container. Some gardeners even grow them in trash cans! While trash bins may not be your garden style, grow bags are a simple, easy-to-store alternative to traditional container gardening, especially if you're short on real estate but are still interested in harvesting your own veggies.

A rule of thumb is that each seed potato needs roughly three gallons of soil to grow a healthy plant, which will produce three to six potatoes to harvest.

YIELD: 30 TO 60 POTATOES

MATERIALS

Seed Potatoes (10)
Try Yukon Gold potatoes for a solid, hearty potato that produces a harvest in fewer than 90 days. Other common varieties include russet and Red Pontiac.

Soil (3 bags, 2 cubic feet each)
Potatoes prefer well-draining, loose soil with a slightly acidic to neutral pH (around 5.8 to 6.5). Amend the soil with organic matter, like compost, to improve fertility and drainage.

Grow Bag (30-gallon bag)
Grow-bags are made with a special fabric that allows the roots and soil to breathe inside the container.

Watering Can or Hose
Potatoes require consistent moisture throughout the growing season, so access to water is essential. Provide regular watering to keep the soil evenly moist but not waterlogged.

Gardening Gloves
Basic gardening gloves will protect your hands and nails when planting and harvesting your potatoes.

Trowel
A trowel will help you to dig up the potatoes when they're ready to harvest.

INSTRUCTIONS

1. **Select Potato Varieties**

   Choose potato varieties suitable for your region and climate. Russet, Yukon Gold, and Red Pontiac are popular choices. You can experiment with different types based on your taste and gardening preferences.

2. **Source Seed Potatoes**

   Buy your certified seed potatoes from a reputable source. These are disease-free and ensure a healthy start for your potato plants. Avoid using potatoes from the grocery store, which may carry diseases or have been treated to prevent sprouting.

3. **Choose Right Time and Place to Plant**

   Potatoes thrive in cool weather. Plant them in early spring, a few weeks before the last expected frost in your area. You can also plant a crop in late summer for a second harvest in the cooler fall. Choose a sunny spot, as potatoes need a minimum of 6 to 8 hours of sunlight each day.

4. **Plant Potatoes in Grow Bag**

   Cut the seed potatoes into chunks, ensuring that each piece has at least one "eye" (sprout). Allow the cut pieces to air-dry for a day or two. When ready to plant, pour well-draining, loose potting mix into the grow bag, until the soil reaches 2 or 3 inches from the top. Then, plant the seed potatoes about 4 to 6 inches deep and 6 inches apart. As the plants grow, mound soil around the stems to encourage tuber development.

5. **Provide Enough Water**

   Make sure that the soil stays consistently moist but not overly saturated. Water deeply whenever the soil feels dry to the touch.

6. **Harvest**

   Early potatoes can be harvested when the plants start flowering, while main crop potatoes are harvested when the tops have completely withered. Use a garden trowel to delicately unearth the tubers. Let the harvested potatoes cure in a cool, dark location for a week before storage.

7. **Store Potatoes**

   Potatoes should be stored in a cool, dark, and well-ventilated place. Avoid storing them in the refrigerator, as the cold temperatures can convert starches into sugars.

Rhubarb

RHEUM OFFICINALE

COMMON NAME: CHINESE RHUBARB

Rhubarb is a vegetable used in varying gardening and culinary traditions. It is a perennial plant that grows large, brightly colored stalks with shades ranging from deep red to pale green. These stalks are the edible part of the plant. The leaves have high levels of oxalic acid and should not be ingested.

Rhubarb's stalks are typically harvested when they reach their full size and vibrant color. The tartness of rhubarb lends itself well to various culinary applications, particularly in desserts and preserves.

NORTHANGER ABBEY

In *Northanger Abbey*, Catherine Morland mentions rhubarb when reflecting on the contradictions of English society and her belief that England caters to a culture in which the "bad" can thrive as much as the "good." Medicinal rhubarb powder was popular during the Regency and readily available at many shops:

> *But in the central part of England there was surely some security for the existence even of a wife not beloved, in the laws of the land, and the manners of the age. Murder was not tolerated, servants were not slaves, and neither poison nor sleeping potions to be procured, like **rhubarb**, from every druggist.*

A SHORT HISTORY OF RHUBARB

Rhubarb boasts a rich history dating back to ancient China, where it was initially grown for its medicinal properties. In traditional Chinese medicine, the plant's roots were prized for their ability to ease digestive issues and enhance general health. Its culinary potential was realized later, as its distinctive flavor and versatility in cooking became appreciated.

Interestingly, rhubarb root became one of the most sought-after medicines of the eighteenth century. It came in powdered form from the East and was mixed with a liquid, like wine, and used to "cure" all kinds of ailments—from rickets to stomach issues.

As sugar became more readily available in England and Europe during the nineteenth century, culinary rhubarb gained use as an ingredient in jams, pies, and other desserts. Its tangy taste offered a delightful contrast to sweet flavors. The cultivation of rhubarb spread to gardens and farms, where it thrived in temperate climates.

Today, rhubarb remains a well-loved ingredient in many recipes worldwide. It is widely available during its peak season in spring and early summer. Rhubarb's tartness adds a refreshing and tangy note to various dishes, and it continues to be a common choice for desserts, sauces, and preserves.

Strawberries

FRAGARIA SPP.

Garden **strawberry** varieties differ in color, shape, and size. The strawberry is known for its edible fruit and is part of the *Fragaria* genus, which includes more than twenty species and even more hybrids.

EMMA

Strawberries are first mentioned in *Emma* as Mrs. Elton and Mr. Knightley converge to create alternate plans for a group exploring trip and picnic:

> *"You had better explore to Donwell," replied Mr. Knightley. "That may be done without horses. Come, and eat my **strawberries**. They are ripening fast."*

*. . . Donwell was famous for its **strawberry**-beds, which seemed a plea for the invitation: but no plea was necessary; cabbage-beds would have been enough to tempt the lady, who only wanted to be going somewhere. . . .*

Mrs. Elton proposes:

*. . . "We are to walk about your gardens, and gather the **strawberries** ourselves, and sit under trees;—and whatever else you may like to provide, it is to be all out of doors—a table spread in the shade, you know. Every thing as natural and simple as possible. Is not that your idea?"*

To which Mr. Knightley replies:

*"Not quite. My idea of the simple and the natural will be to have the table spread in the dining-room. The nature and the simplicity of gentlemen and ladies, with their servants and furniture, I think is best observed by meals within doors. When you are tired of eating **strawberries** in the garden, there shall be cold meat in the house."*

Later, when plans for the outing to Box Hill were confirmed, the group gathers before setting out and talks about strawberries, highlighting how important they were to the culinary tastes and status:

*These were pleasant feelings, and she walked about and indulged them till it was necessary to do as the others did, and collect round the **strawberry**-beds. The whole party were assembled, excepting Frank Churchill, who was expected every moment from Richmond; and Mrs. Elton, in all her apparatus of happiness, her large bonnet and her basket, was very ready to lead the way in gathering, accepting, or talking—**strawberries**, and only **strawberries**, could now be thought or spoken of.—"The best fruit in England—every body's favorite—always wholesome.—These the finest beds and finest sorts.—Delightful to gather for one's self—the only way of really enjoying them.—Morning decidedly the best time—never tired—every sort good—hautboy infinitely superior—no comparison—the others hardly eatable—hautboys very scarce—Chili preferred—white wood finest* *flavor of all—price of **strawberries** in London—abundance about Bristol—Maple Grove—cultivation—beds when to be renewed—gardeners thinking exactly different—no general rule—gardeners never to be put out of their way—delicious fruit—only too rich to be eaten much of—inferior to cherries—currants more refreshing—only objection to gathering **strawberries** the stooping—glaring sun—tired to death—could bear it no longer—must go and sit in the shade."*

Once the party arrives at Box Hill, Emma teases Frank Churchill for his tardiness:

"How much I am obliged to you," said [Frank Churchill], "for telling me to come to-day!—If it had not been for you, I should certainly have lost all the happiness of this party. I had quite determined to go away again."

*"Yes, you were very cross; and I do not know what about, except that you were too late for the best **strawberries**. I was a kinder friend than you deserved. But you were humble. You begged hard to be commanded to come."*

A SHORT HISTORY OF STRAWBERRIES

Small, native strawberries thrive in English landscapes, with their roots back hundreds if not thousands of years. However, it wasn't until the 1500s that a significant shift occurred with the introduction of the American *Fragaria virginiana,* known as the Virginia strawberry. This newcomer brought a tantalizing twist to the table, offering a taste superior to the diminutive wild berries that had long been cultivated.

Strawberries underwent a remarkable transformation through the meticulous process of crossbreeding during the eighteenth and nineteenth centuries. This diligent effort bore fruit, quite literally, as plump, luscious strawberries emerged as the new standard. Varieties like *Fragaria moschata* and *Fragaria ×ananassa* rose to prominence, captivating growers and consumers alike with their sweetness and juiciness.

Today, the legacy of strawberries endures, transcending seasons as they grace the shelves of grocery markets year-round. In England, the affinity for these delectable berries remains steadfast, epitomized by the cherished tradition at Wimbledon, where strawberries and cream have been savored since 1877. Across the nation, festivals pay homage to the strawberry, commemorating its integral role in England's agricultural heritage and uniting communities in celebration of this beloved fruit.

CULTIVATING JANE

Grow Strawberries in Hanging Baskets

Growing strawberries in hanging baskets on a balcony or patio offers an opportunity to cultivate your own fresh homegrown berries even if you don't have space for a full-blown kitchen garden.

YIELD: 1 HANGING BASKET OF STRAWBERRY PLANTS

MATERIALS

Strawberry Plants (12 seedlings)
It's essential to source disease-free strawberry plants from a reputable nursery or garden center. Select plants that are well suited for container gardening, such as everbearing or day-neutral varieties. These are typically sold in small, 3-inch plastic nursery pots.

Hanging Strawberry Planter (1)
Hanging strawberry planters come in a variety of styles, ranging from simple bags to more decorative ceramic options. These planters have holes that allow the plants to grow through the sides and drape downward. A hanging planter with at least 12 holes for planting will give you the best harvest. More holes mean more strawberries! These

planters are also designed to be planted with each seedling going in above the previous one, with a layer of soil in between.

Potting Mix (2 cubic feet)

Strawberries grow well in easy-draining, slightly acidic soil. A potting mix designed for berries or fruits will have these qualities, ensuring proper aeration, drainage, and nutrient availability for the strawberry plants.

Watering Can or Hose

Strawberries require consistent moisture, especially during flowering and fruiting.

Berry Fertilizer (4-pound bag)

This type of fertilizer is specifically created to enhance plant growth and berry production.

Garden Shears

To help cut back the plants' runners, if necessary.

Organic Insecticidal Spray (as necessary)

Natural bug repellants can help keep insects from devouring your plants. You can make your own with essential oils, like lemongrass and rosemary, which are much better for you and the environment than the arsenic-based insecticides used during the Regency era.

INSTRUCTIONS

1. **Plant Strawberries**

   Plant strawberry seedlings in the spring for an early summer harvest. To plant a strawberry hanger, follow these steps:
   - Fill the hanger with soil up to the first planting hole.
   - Gently pat down the soil.

- Remove the plant from its container and place it in the hole, ensuring all foliage is outside the hanger.
- Add potting mix until you reach the next set of holes, then repeat the process.

2. Provide Adequate Sunlight

Strawberries flourish when exposed to full sunlight. Ensure your hanging planter is positioned in an area that receives a minimum of 6 to 8 hours of direct sunlight daily.

3. Water

Keep the soil consistently moist, especially during the growing season and when the plants are producing fruit.

4. Fertilize

Fertilize strawberries regularly with a balanced, water-soluble fertilizer. Follow the instructions on the packaging, and avoid overfertilizing, which leads to excessive foliage growth and hinders fruit production.

5. Pinch Runners

Using your fingers or garden shears to remove or "pinch off" long stems, called runners. This will help the plant to produce more fruit.

6. Pest Control

Watch out for prevalent pests, such as aphids and slugs. Remove any slugs that have made their way onto your plants, and if you find any other tiny, plant-sucking insects, use an organic insecticidal spray to deter them.

7. Harvest

Harvest strawberries when they have reached their peak color, which is typically a deep shade of red—though each variety may vary. Pick them gently to avoid damaging the delicate fruit. Regular harvesting helps the plant to produce more berries.

THE
CONSERVATORY

The Georgian era and the Regency period were characterized by a combination of societal refinement, scientific curiosity, and a fascination with the exotic. Within this cultural melting pot, conservatories quickly gained favor as glass-enclosed marvels, encapsulating both horticultural splendor and architectural beauty. These structures were more than mere storage for plants; they were symbols of status, social spaces for entertainment, and embodiments of the era's botanical and colonial fixations.

At the heart of the conservatory's appeal was its role as a showcase for horticultural delights. Akin to curated galleries of the natural world, these glass sanctuaries exhibited exotic plant collections that had been acquired through the explorations of intrepid botanists and adventurers. Possessing such a botanical menagerie became a tangible marker of wealth and prestige, a testament to one's ability to procure rare specimens and nurture them within the conservatory's controlled environment.

Beyond their botanical function, conservatories were architectural marvels, designed to catch the eye while blending seamlessly with the natural world. Their glass walls allowed sunlight to filter through, creating a luminous and inviting atmosphere. Adorned with decorative ironwork, these structures became aesthetic focal points, enhancing the elegance of the estates that housed them.

Conservatories also served as social spaces, providing a picturesque backdrop for gatherings and entertainment. The lush greenery within created an enchanting setting for teas, conversations, and—as the literature of the time reflects—romantic retreats. The glass walls blurred the lines between indoor and outdoor spaces, allowing hosts to bring the beauty of nature into the heart of their homes.

A practical innovation of conservatories was their role in extending the growing season. In an era when agriculture depended on the whims of weather, the glass-enclosed spaces offered a controlled environment for year-round gardening. The ability to cultivate plants that would otherwise succumb to the harshness of English winters became a testament to the ingenuity of the era's landowners.

Scientific curiosity thrived within the conservatory's walls. As the Regency era embraced botanical studies and scientific exploration, these spaces provided a chance to observe plant behavior, conduct experiments, and advance horticultural knowledge. The conservatory became a living laboratory wherein the intersection of scientific inquiry and aesthetic appreciation flourished.

The ownership of a conservatory, with its associated costs and maintenance, was also a symbol of societal standing. Reserved for the elite class, these structures were expressions of refined taste and cultural capital. They also came to represent British imperialism, showcasing the allure of so-called "exotic" plants and specimens imported from distant parts of the British Empire.

EXPLORING GREENHOUSE AND CONSERVATORY OPTIONS FOR YOUR GARDEN

Would you like to extend your growing season and add a beautiful focal point to your garden? A greenhouse or conservatory can be a special addition to your garden. With various styles and sizes to choose from, you can find the perfect structure for your needs, climate, and space. You can even opt for a convenient greenhouse kit, ranging from small to large, for an easy and efficient assembly process. These greenhouses are reminiscent of the grand glasshouses of the Regency era. Today, you can bring a touch of that elegance to your own garden as well.

1. WINDOWPANE GREENHOUSES

Constructed using reclaimed windowpanes, these greenhouses offer a charming vintage aesthetic. They can be custom sized to fit your garden space, making them unique and personalized additions.

2. HOOP HOUSES

Simple and cost-effective, hoop houses are made from PVC pipes or metal hoops covered with plastic sheeting. Easy to assemble and disassemble, they're perfect for seasonal growing and can be easily relocated.

3. COLD FRAMES

Small and low-cost, cold frames are ideal for starting seeds and protecting plants. Typically made from plastic or wood and glass or plastic, they harness the sun's energy to create a warm microclimate, extending the growing season and allowing for earlier planting.

4. LEAN-TO GREENHOUSES

Attached to an existing building, lean-to greenhouses share the building's heat and space, making them an efficient and practical option. Ideal for smaller areas, they provide convenient access and energy efficiency.

5. MINI GREENHOUSES

Compact and portable, mini greenhouses are perfect for small spaces, like balconies or patios. Great for growing herbs, vegetables, and flowers, they offer an easy and affordable way to start gardening, even with limited space.

JANE'S REGENCY CONSERVATORIES AND GLASSHOUSES

Jane lived during a time when conservatories and glasshouses were part of the architectural landscape. During her lifetime, she likely would have visited some notable conservatories associated with grand estates and public gardens.

CHATSWORTH HOUSE

During the Regency era, Chatsworth House in Derbyshire, then owned by William Cavendish, the 6th Duke of Devonshire, retained its grandeur and cultural significance. The renowned gardens, designed by Capability Brown under the 4th Duke, continued to flourish, with orangeries and conservatories showcasing exotic flora. The estate's architectural features, both inside and out, reflected the classical Georgian style, with occasional updates to align with contemporary design trends. As a social and cultural hub, Chatsworth hosted various events, drawing interest from the literary world, as evidenced by visits from authors, like Jane, who is thought to have visited in 1811 during her stay in Bakewell. There is much speculation among literary scholars and historians that Pemberley in *Pride and Prejudice* was based on Chatsworth, though there is no official proof.

Later, in 1840, The Great Conservatory opened at Chatsworth under the watchful eye and design of famed horticulturalist Joseph Paxton. Upon opening, it became the largest glasshouse in the world.

HAMPTON COURT PALACE

Situated on the outskirts of London, Hampton Court Palace boasted expansive gardens during the Regency era. Within these grounds, a notable feature was the Great Vine, which still thrives as the world's oldest and largest grapevine. Planted in 1768 by Capability Brown, it thrived within a greenhouse on the palace premises and garnered significant attention as a tourist attraction.

BLENHEIM PALACE

Blenheim Palace in Oxfordshire, a UNESCO World Heritage Site, features impressive gardens redesigned by—who else?—Capability Brown. During the Regency era, Blenheim had a large conservatory that was called The Orangery. George Spencer, 4th Duke of Marlborough, turned it into a theater for his children to put on plays—but it was restored to its original use as a plant conservatory. These days, the space functions as The Orangery restaurant, where visitors of Blenheim Palace can experience fine dining in a truly historical setting.

THE ROYAL PAVILION, BRIGHTON

Built for the prince regent (later George IV) during the 1780s, the Royal Pavilion in Brighton was known for its exotic architecture and interiors. The gardens included structures to house all kinds of tropical plants.

KENSINGTON GARDENS

Kensington Gardens, part of Hyde Park in London, had an orangery during the Regency era. While not as grand as some conservatories that would come later, it was a space for cultivating citrus trees and tender plants.

SYDNEY GARDENS

Opened in 1795, Sydney Gardens in Bath were public pleasure gardens featuring walks, water features, and entertainment. When the Austens lived in Bath, Jane frequently used the gardens. Although it did not have a large conservatory, it likely had structures for showcasing and protecting delicate plants.

BICTON PARK BOTANICAL GARDENS

Bicton Park in Devon is home to one of the oldest conservatories in England. The Palm House was built in the 1820s at the tail end of the Regency and is widely considered one of the most detailed intact examples of glasshouse architecture. The conservatory is constructed of roughly eighteen thousand glass panes on a cast-iron frame.

CULTIVATING JANE

Create a Tablescape with Conservatory Fruit

Step back in time and create an elegant tablescape worthy of a gathering at Pemberley or Hartfield. Drawing inspiration from the delicate blooms and succulent fruits that could be found growing in the conservatories of Jane's novels, this endeavor captures the essence of Regency charm.

YIELD: THE MATERIALS LISTED WILL NICELY ADORN A
STANDARD 6-FOOT DINING TABLE, BUT THE PROJECT CAN EASILY
BE MODIFIED TO SUIT ANY SURFACE SIZE.

MATERIALS

Lace or Linen
Use lace or linen fabric as a tablecloth or table runner to provide a soft and elegant backdrop.

Small Vases or Bowls (3 to 5)
If available, use elegant crystal or silver vases or bowls to display the flowers and fruits.

Clear Tape (1 roll)
Use clear tape as a grid for larger floral arrangements.

Garden Shears
Use garden shears to cut and trim the greenery and flower stems to the desired length for arranging in vases or bowls.

Assorted Fresh-Cut Greenery (25 to 30 stems)

Select various types of fresh-cut greenery to complement the flowers. Ivy, myrtle, boxwood, fern, and
rosemary are all excellent choices.

Assorted Fresh-Cut Flowers (15 to 20 stems)

Choose a variety of fresh-cut flowers typical of the
Regency era, such as roses, violets, hyacinths, and
sweet peas.

Fabric Scissors

Use fabric scissors to trim your ribbons.

Ribbons (3 to 5 yards)

Select delicate ribbons in a variety of shades to add decorative
accents to the tablescape.

Fruits (6 to 10)

Include fruits that could be found in the Regency era, such as citrus fruits, pineapples,
grapes, or any hothouse fruits. These fruits add both visual appeal and authenticity to
the tablescape.

Posy Bouquets (4 to 6)

Follow the instructions on page 33 to make your own!

Taper Candles, Candlesticks, Votives, and/or Tealights (3 to 5) (optional)

Use taper candles in silver or crystal candlesticks to create an ambient lighting effect.

INSTRUCTIONS

1. **Create Space**

   Clear your table and lay down the linens you'd like to use for a tablecloth or runner.

2. **Prepare Vases**

   Clean your vessels with hot water and soap. After they dry, make a grid along the tops of the vases with clear tape. This will act as your support as you build your floral design. Fill the vases with water.

3. **Trim and Arrange Greenery**

   Trim your greenery to the desired lengths and arrange it evenly around a vase through the holes in the grid. This will provide the foundation for your floral arrangement.

4. **Arrange Flowers**

   Start with the larger blooms, like roses. Trim the stems to the desired length and place them throughout the grid into the vase. Incorporate smaller blooms, like violets or sweet peas, to add texture and variety. Distribute them evenly for a balanced look. Add more greenery, if needed.

5. **Tie with Ribbons**

   Wrap a delicate ribbon around the vase, tying it in a bow for a touch of Regency-era refinement.

6. **Repeat**

   Repeat steps 3, 4, and 5 with all of your vases. For variety, try to make each arrangement slightly different from the last with variations of color and size and a variety of blooms and greenery.

7. **Place**

   Place your vases along the table. Spread them out or group them as your vision guides you!

8. **Display Fruit**

   Position fruits of various sizes around the floral arrangements or in separate bowls.

9. **Add Greenery Accents**

   Weave sprigs of greenery into the floral arrangements so that they drape out onto the table. Place additional greenery around the base of each arrangement or intertwine with the fruits.

10. **Arrange Individual Flower Posies**

    Prepare individual flower posies (see page 33). Place one at each setting for a personal touch.

11. **Enhance with Candlelight (optional)**

    Arrange taper candles in silver or crystal candlesticks down the center of the table. Consider adding votive candles or tea lights for additional ambiance.

Geranium

PELARGONIUM SPP.

Pelargoniums—which are commonly, and incorrectly, called **geraniums**—comprise a diverse genus of flowering plants encompassing approximately 280 varieties. These range from small to medium-sized perennials, annuals, and larger shrubs. (Interestingly, the name "geranium" technically belongs to an unrelated genus of plants commonly known as cranesbills, several of which are indigenous to England.)

Pelargoniums are prized for their delicate blossoms, borne on elongated stems that gracefully arch away from the plant. Their green leaves are typically lobed, varying in texture from hairy to smooth, and sometimes display diverse coloration. Certain varieties, dubbed "scented geraniums," boast leaves with potent fragrances reminiscent of apple, lavender, lemon, orange, and more.

Jane likely referred to pelargoniums when mentioning geraniums in her writings, as the South African pelargoniums were commonly imported to England during her time. This contrasts with the native English geranium that would have been found in the wild on the grounds of estates like Mansfield Park.

MANSFIELD PARK

Fanny Price, confused at how to understand Edmund Bertram, considers how to gain a bit of "mental strength" so that she might be able to make a choice. She wonders if giving her "geraniums" a breath of fresh air would also help her own mentality:

> To this nest of comforts Fanny now walked down to try its influence on an agitated, doubting spirit, to see if by looking at Edmund's profile she could catch any of his counsel, or by giving air to her **geraniums** she might inhale a breeze of mental strength herself.

A SHORT HISTORY OF THE PELARGONIUM

Pelargoniums originated in South Africa and traveled across continents and centuries, ultimately establishing themselves as one of the most fashionable plants in European hothouses by the late 1700s. Initially introduced to Europe (likely via the Netherlands) in the early 1600s, they found their way to England and Germany from France, captivating botanists and hobby collectors alike with their diverse varieties and ease of cultivation.

Despite their South African roots, pelargoniums bore a striking resemblance to the native cranesbill geranium, leading to widespread confusion and the adoption of the misnomer "geranium." This linguistic mix-up endured over time, solidifying the interchangeability of "pelargonium" and "geranium," a convention still observed today.

Against the backdrop of Regency England's aesthetic of informality, pelargoniums transitioned from hothouses to indoor settings, becoming a favored houseplant among the upper class throughout the eighteenth and nineteenth centuries. Adorned with scented leaves, certain varieties found additional popularity, serving dual purposes in aromatic sachets, potpourri, and even scenting the water in finger bowls.

In contemporary gardening, pelargoniums continue to shine, adorning garden beds, hanging baskets, and containers with their vibrant hues throughout the warmer seasons. Their versatility extends to indoor cultivation during winter, only to be reintroduced outdoors come spring. Thanks to extensive hybridization efforts, pelargoniums now boast an array of shapes, sizes, and colors.

Grapes

VITIS SPP.

The **grapevine** is a deciduous, fast-growing plant. With good conditions, it can quickly reach thirty to forty feet in length. Grapes, depending on the species, can be round or oval and come in shades of green, purple, or red.

PRIDE AND PREJUDICE

When they visit Pemberley, Elizabeth Bennet and her aunt are offered heaps of fruit, including grapes. Through the narration, Jane hints that such delicacies as grapes require a hothouse—an expensive luxury:

*The next variation which their visit afforded was produced by the entrance of servants with cold meat, cake, and a variety of all the finest fruits in season; but this did not take place till after many a significant look and smile from Mrs. Annesley to Miss Darcy had been given, to remind her of her post. There was now employment for the whole party—for though they could not all talk, they could all eat; and the beautiful pyramids of **grapes**, nectarines, and peaches soon collected them round the table.*

A SHORT HISTORY OF GRAPES

Grapes have been grown and utilized since the Neolithic period. Ancient Mesopotamians, Greeks, and Egyptians all used grapes in some way, from wine to medicine.

In England, archaeologists unearthed evidence of grape growth dating back to prehistoric times, and grapes were imported to England even before the Romans crossed the English Channel.

During the Georgian and Regency periods, grapes became symbols of wealth and status because, in England, one could only grow them year-round with a hothouse. After harvesting, the fruits were used to create massive, sometimes table-long centerpieces, to which guests would help themselves. The attractiveness of grapes even spurred the invention of grape shears—a delicate pair of long-handled scissors that were used to cut clusters of grapes away from the centerpiece and onto one's plate.

Grapes are still favored, of course, and—thankfully—no longer require special utensils to enjoy. Table grapes have been hybridized to multiple tastes, shapes, and consistencies. One of the most popular grapes of the twenty-first century has been the Cotton Candy grape, a hybrid between Concord and California grapes that snaps in the mouth like a sugary treat.

Hyacinth

HYACINTHUS SPP.

The **hyacinth** is a fragrant genus of bulb plant that belongs to the same family as aspara-gus, Asparagaceae, formerly known as Hyacinthaceae. There are three official species of hyacinth: *Hyacinthus litwinovii, Hyacinthus orientalis*—the most common, also known as the Dutch hyacinth or common hyacinth—and *Hyanthis transcaspicus.*

Hyacinths are a favorite of the spring-blooming bulbs but can technically be forced—or coaxed—to grow indoors or in a greenhouse at any time of year. The bulbs bloom in various colors, although the Dutch hyacinth's royal shades of blue and purple have historically been the most preferred.

NORTHANGER ABBEY

During her first morning at Northanger Abbey, Catherine Morland comes to breakfast and finds that Henry Tilney is already there. To keep him from teasing her about her fears from the night before, she changes the subject to focus on the potted hyacinths in the breakfast room. Catherine's arrival at Northanger Abbey takes place in March, which means that the hyacinths were likely planted in pots or displayed in bulb glasses, which was fashionable at the time:

*". . . What beautiful **hyacinths**! I have just learnt to love a **hyacinth**."*

"And how might you learn? By accident or argument?"

"Your sister taught me; I cannot tell how. Mrs. Allen used to take pains, year after year, to make me like them; but I never could, till I saw them the other day in Milsom Street; I am naturally indifferent about flowers."

*"But now you love a **hyacinth**. So much the better. You have gained a new source of enjoyment, and it is well to have as many holds upon happiness as possible. Besides, a taste for flowers is always desirable in your sex, as a means of getting you out of doors, and tempting you to more frequent exercise than you would otherwise take. And though the love of a **hyacinth** may be rather domestic, who can tell, the sentiment once raised, but you may in time come to love a rose?"*

A SHORT HISTORY OF HYACINTHS

Hyacinths are native to Asia and the eastern Mediterranean and have been in cultivation for thousands of years, even figuring in the works of Homer, Ovid, Virgil, and other ancient authors. But it wasn't until the sixteenth century that the flower became accessible in western Europe and captured the attention of prominent English gardeners.

In Regency-era garden design, hyacinths were highly valued for their blooms and intense fragrance. They were often planted in large clumps, sometimes in flower-beds and other times in pots set along a gravel walk, terrace, or balcony. The flowers were often included in indoor arrangements, and during the Regency, when hyacinth bulbs were very rare and expensive, they came to signify wealth and status.

Today, hyacinths still symbolize the arrival of spring and the end of winter, and they have become one of the most readily available spring bulbs and among the easiest to grow. Although hyacinths thrive when planted outdoors in garden beds during the growing season, they also excel as container plants. Ideal for porches or balconies, these versatile, compact flowers bring beauty to any outdoor space. Hyacinths are also commonly forced to bloom indoors during the winter and early spring in containers or water vases.

Peaches and Nectarines

PRUNUS PERSICA AND *PRUNUS PERSICA* VAR. *NUCIPERSICA*

Nectarines and **peaches** are almost identical, with just one genetic difference. Due to the natural hybridization that can occur over time, nectarines are smooth-skinned, while peaches sport a soft fuzz. Many people think of nectarines as a separate species from the peach, but they are not. The only thing that scientifically distinguishes the peach from the nectarine is one gene that grows fuzz on the fruit's skin. It's even quite common for a rogue mutation to cause nectarines and peaches to grow on the same tree.

PRIDE AND PREJUDICE

In *Pride and Prejudice*, "pyramids" of exotic fruit are served alongside other delicacies at Pemberley when Elizabeth visits after being convinced that Miss Bingley is jealous of her. "Grapes, **nectarines**, and **peaches**" are among the impressive display. (See page 76 for the complete excerpt.)

A SHORT HISTORY OF PEACHES AND NECTARINES

Although the botanical name *Prunus persica* translates to "Persian plum," nectarines and peaches came to England by way of China, where they were grown as early as 6000 BC. Through the Silk Road trade routes, the trees ended up in Persia, Greece, and Rome. It's commonly believed that Alexander the Great brought peaches and nectarines to Europe, but they didn't begin to appear on English tables until the seventeenth century. First grown by the upper classes as expensive and exotic fruits, it wasn't until the mid-1900s that peaches and nectarines became more common.

Equally prized in garden design, peach and nectarine trees were often forced to grow in fan shapes—also known as espalier—against a wall or trained into arches on trellises to create a decorative focal feature. They could also be found growing in kitchen gardens, and the tree's blossoms were often used in floral arrangements around the home. Most importantly, as in the reference from *Pride and Prejudice*, they could be grown in conservatories and hothouses, producing fruit for the household even when they were out of season.

Today, peaches and nectarines are grown for the commercial value of their fruit and for their use in garden design. Although they're no longer such rare delicacies, nectarines and peaches remain beloved treats, consumed in desserts, salads, pizzas, and more.

Pineapple

ANANAS COMOSUS

The **pineapple** plant is a slow-growing perennial that sprouts thirty to forty succulent leaves in an alternating pattern along its thick stem. The plant often doesn't produce fruit until two or three years after planting.

A flower stalk will appear, and after pollination, the flowers (along with the bracts that attach them to the stalk) become fleshy and begin to form the pineapple fruit. Once the fruit forms, it takes about six months to ripen enough for harvest.

NORTHANGER ABBEY

The pineapple reference appears inconspicuously in *Northanger Abbey* with the word "pinery." A pinery is a hothouse used for the cultivation of pineapple plants and the production of their fruit. During a tour of the Northanger Abbey gardens, General Tilney boasts of his wealth but admits that all his money and resources could not promise a successful harvest from the pinery:

> *The number of acres contained in this garden was such as Catherine could not listen to without dismay, being more than double the extent of all Mr. Allen's, as well as her father's, including church-yard and orchard. The walls seemed count-less in number, endless in length; a village of hot-houses seemed to arise among them, and a whole parish to be at work within the enclosure. The general was flattered by her looks of surprise, which told him almost as plainly, as he soon forced her to tell him in words, that she had never seen any gardens at all equal to them before; and he then modestly owned that, "without any ambition of that sort himself—without any solicitude about it—he did believe them to be unrivalled in the kingdom. If he had a hobby-horse, it was that. He loved a garden. Though careless enough in most matters of eating, he loved good fruit—or if he did not, his friends and children did. There were great vexations, however, attending such a garden as his. The utmost care could not always secure the most valuable fruits. The **pinery** had yielded only one hundred in the last year. Mr. Allen, he supposed, must feel these inconveniences as well as himself."*

A SHORT HISTORY OF PINEAPPLES

The earliest European encounters with pineapples were those of Christopher Columbus and later Sir Walter Raleigh, who stumbled upon the fruit flourishing in the West Indies. Native to modern-day Brazil and Paraguay, pineapples were a well-established crop in the Americas. The fruit's exotic allure captured the imagination of Europeans, prompt-ing its introduction to the continent and its swift export to various tropical regions around the world.

As the pineapple's popularity soared, so did advancements in horticultural technology, encouraging cultivation in temperate climates. Despite the initial expense, by the time of the Regency era, English gardeners were able to nurture sizable pineapple crops within the confines of hothouses, aided by skilled gardeners.

Since then, the pineapple has undergone a remarkable transformation in accessibility and availability. No longer an extravagant luxury reserved for the elite, advancements in agricultural practices, coupled with the proliferation of pineapple farms in tropical regions worldwide, have rendered this once-costly fruit far more affordable and available year-round.

CULTIVATING JANE
Make Citrus Pomanders

A pomander is a fragrant ball or perforated container filled with aromatic substances, such as herbs, spices, or essential oils. Historically, it was used to ward off foul odors, protect against disease, or provide a pleasant scent in enclosed spaces, like rooms, closets, or drawers. Pomanders were prevalent during the Renaissance and Victorian eras and were often made from materials like oranges, lemons, cloves, or other aromatic spices.

These fragrant wonders, both fashionable and functional, were cherished during the Regency for their intricate designs and aromatic allure. They adorned drawing rooms and wardrobes and served as fashionable tokens of elegance and refinement. In this DIY guide, we'll explore the art of creating your own pomanders, infusing your space with the timeless charm and sophistication of the Regency era.

MATERIALS

Toothpick or Skewer (1)

A toothpick or skewer is used to create a design on the surface of the citrus fruit before inserting the cloves. This design can guide the placement of the cloves and add artistic flair to the pomander.

Citrus Fruit (1)

An orange or other citrus fruit will serve as the base for the pomander. Choose a fruit that is firm and without blemishes, as it will hold its shape better during the crafting process and maintain its appearance over time. While the size is a matter of preference, smaller fruits often work best for pomanders.

Cloves (1 to 2 ounces)

Cloves are the primary ingredient used to scent the pomander. They are inserted into the peel of the citrus fruit in decorative patterns, creating a visually appealing design and pleasant aroma.

Ribbon or Lace (1 yard)

Ribbon or lace is used to embellish the pomander, adding a decorative element to the finished product.

Decorative Pins (2 to 3)

Decorative pins are used to secure the ribbon or lace onto the pomander.

INSTRUCTIONS

1. **Create Design**

   Use the toothpick or skewer to delicately etch a design onto the fruit's peel. This design will guide the placement of the cloves. The traditional Regency pomander often featured intricate patterns, ranging from geometric shapes to fully covered surfaces. Don't be afraid to get elaborate!

2. **Insert Cloves**

   Gently push the pointed ends of the cloves into the fruit along the design lines or pattern you've created. This process, though time-consuming, is both therapeutic and rewarding, resulting in a visually stunning and fragrant masterpiece.

3. **Decorate with Ribbon or Lace**

   Embrace the ornate aesthetic of the Regency era by adorning your pomander with ribbon or lace. You can make small bows or wrap ribbon or lace around the fruit. Use decorative pins to secure them in place.

4. **Create Hanging Loop**

   If you desire a hanging pomander, loop a longer piece of ribbon or lace through the pinned ribbon sections from the previous step and tie it securely at the top.

5. **Allow to Cure**

   Begin the preservation process by placing your pomander in a cool, dry location for several weeks. This curing period enhances both the longevity of the fruit and the intensity of its aroma.

6. **Display or Gift**

   Once cured, display your pomander in a bowl, hang it in your closet, or consider giving it to a friend.

THE
PARKLAND

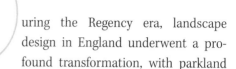

uring the Regency era, landscape design in England underwent a profound transformation, with parkland emerging as a continued symbol of wealth, status, and artistic innovation. Here, "parkland" or "park" refers to expansive estates or grounds surrounding grand country houses or manors. These areas were typically landscaped and designed to showcase the wealth and status of their owners while also providing spaces for leisure, recreation, and aesthetic appreciation.

Parkland during the Regency often included manicured lawns, woodlands, lakes, ornamental gardens, outdoor recreational areas, and architectural follies, like ornamental temples, "ruins," or towers. These landscapes were meticulously planned and carefully cultivated by landscape architects and head gardeners to create harmonious compositions that blended seamlessly with the natural surroundings.

The expansive estates became not only showcases of the aristocracy's prosperity but also canvases for leading landscape architects, like Capability Brown and Humphry Repton.

The evolution of these spaces was characterized by a departure from the formal geometric layouts of previous periods toward a more naturalistic approach that aimed to emulate the beauty of untouched nature. This shift in perspective reflected broader cultural and philosophical changes, with Romanticism influencing attitudes toward the landscape and the sublime beauty of the natural world.

At the heart of Regency parkland design was the concept of the picturesque—a term popularized by landscape theorist and writer William Gilpin—which emphasized the creation of visually striking scenes that evoked a sense of awe and wonder. To achieve this, designers employed a range of techniques, from the strategic placement of trees and shrubs to the creation of winding paths and artificial lakes, all carefully orchestrated to enhance the overall aesthetic appeal of the landscape.

As we know, one of the key figures in shaping Regency parkland was Capability Brown, whose visionary approach to landscape design revolutionized the field. Brown's landscapes, characterized by sweeping vistas and rolling lawns, are some of the best-known representations of the picturesque style. His work at iconic estates, such as Blenheim Palace and Chatsworth House, set a new standard for landscape architecture and established him as one of the era's most influential parkland designers.

Building on Brown's legacy, Humphry Repton further refined the principles of landscape design. A gifted communicator, Repton delivered his design proposals to clients in the form of elaborate, red leather–bound books that contained detailed descriptions, watercolor representations, and before-and-after overlays. These impressive "Red Books," as they became known, persuaded many estate owners to implement Repton's plans. His parkland designs often featured dramatic focal points, such as architectural follies and ornamental gardens, designed to capture the imagination and create memorable experiences for visitors.

One of the most remarkable features of Regency parkland was its ability to evoke a sense of drama and surprise. Visitors would often encounter carefully framed views as they wandered through the landscape, with each turn revealing a new vista or hidden gem. Architectural elements, such as Gothic ruins or classical temples, served as focal points, drawing the eye and inviting contemplation.

Beyond their aesthetic appeal, Regency parklands were also functional spaces designed for leisure and recreation. They provided opportunities for outdoor pursuits, such as hunting, fishing, and horseback riding, allowing the aristocracy to indulge in their favorite pastimes while surrounded by the beauty of nature. Grand events, including picnics, outdoor concerts, and elaborate garden parties, were common occurrences, providing occasions for socializing and entertaining on a lavish scale.

The creation and maintenance of parkland became a matter of pride and prestige for landowners, who spared no expense in their efforts to enhance the beauty and diversity of their estates. The design and upkeep of these estates spoke volumes about the wealth and refinement of their owners, reinforcing their position at the top of society. Today, many still exist in their glory as enduring reminders of an era defined by elegance, refinement, and the pursuit of taming nature.

REGENCY-ERA WOODLAND MANAGEMENT TECHNIQUES

In Jane Austen's time, woodland management was a critical aspect of estate maintenance. Landowners needed to balance three key goals: generating income from timber and resources, preserving the natural environment, and creating scenic landscapes that enhanced the estate's beauty. This delicate balance was a common topic of conversation among the gentry and landowners, including the Austens, as they traveled and socialized, sharing knowledge and best practices to maintain their estates' prosperity and charm. The following seven methods are still used today to maintain healthy and productive woodlands, providing sustainable resources and enhancing the natural beauty of the landscape. From traditional practices like coppicing and pollarding to innovative approaches like plantation forestry and wood pasturing, these techniques showcase the ingenuity of Regency-era woodland management:

1. COPPICING

Coppicing involved periodically cutting trees down to their stumps to promote the growth of multiple new shoots. This method was commonly used for producing sustainable supplies of wood for fuel, fencing, and building materials. Woods like hazel, ash, and willow were particularly suited for coppicing.

2. POLLARDING

Similar to coppicing, pollarding involved cutting trees back to the trunk at a height of around 6 to 10 feet. This technique was often used in areas where livestock grazed, as it protected the regrowth from being eaten. Pollarded trees produced a regular supply of wood and were commonly seen with species like ash and oak.

3. TIMBER STAND IMPROVEMENT

This technique involved selectively thinning a forest to remove weaker or undesirable trees, allowing the remaining trees to grow stronger and faster. This practice improved the overall quality of timber and enhanced the aesthetic appeal of the woodland.

4. PLANTATION FORESTRY

During this period, planting new trees, especially faster-growing species, became more common. Landowners established plantations of trees like larch, Scots pine, and beech, which were valued for their timber.

5. WOOD PASTURE

Wood pasturing combined forestry and grazing by allowing livestock to graze within wooded areas. This method helped manage underbrush and pro- vided a sustainable system of land use that produced both timber and pasture.

6. SELECTIVE FELLING

Selective felling involved carefully choosing and cutting specific trees to harvest, rather than clear-cutting an entire area. This method ensured continuous forest cover and promoted a diverse age structure within the woodland, main- taining ecological balance.

7. CHARCOAL PRODUCTION

Charcoal production was a significant activity during the Regency. Woods like oak, ash, and hazel were burned in pits or kilns to produce charcoal, which was a vital fuel for various industries, including iron smelting and domestic heating.

JANE'S PARKLANDS

During her frequent travels, Jane would have had access to and likely visited various parklands and estates typical of the Regency era. Some parklands from Jane's era include:

CHAWTON HOUSE

Located in Hampshire, just down the street from the cottage where she lived with her mother and sister, Chawton House was owned by Jane Austen's brother Edward Knight. Jane spent the last eight years of her life in Chawton, where she would have been able to take in and enjoy the parklands of the the Chawton House estate.

GODMERSHAM PARK

Another estate owned by Edward, Godmersham Park in Kent, boasted extensive parkland and gardens designed by renowned landscape architect Capability Brown. Jane visited Godmersham on numerous occasions—for a cumulative ten months—and would have appreciated the beauty of its landscaped grounds.

CHATSWORTH HOUSE

Located in Derbyshire, Chatsworth House is one of England's most famous country estates, known for its extensive parkland, also landscaped by Capability Brown. While there is no definitive evidence that Jane toured the home in 1811 while she was staying in Bakewell, it is likely she did visit, and she would have walked the grounds and admired the vast parklands—perhaps gathering inspiration for Permberley!

BLENHEIM PALACE

Situated in Oxfordshire, Blenheim Palace—yet another majestic design by Capability Brown—is renowned for its magnificent Baroque architecture and sprawling parkland. Jane might have visited this grand estate during her visits to Oxfordshire or nearby areas. If she did not visit, she certainly would have heard of the estate, as it was famed throughout England, much like Chatsworth House.

Many other estates in Hampshire and neighboring counties would have also been accessible to Jane during her travels, offering opportunities for leisurely walks, picnics, and social gatherings in the idyllic surroundings. While specific records of her visits to these estates do not exist, it is likely she explored them.

CULTIVATING JANE

Craft a Decorative Garland

Try your hand at creating a Regency-era garland inspired by the majestic trees that graced the landscapes of grand parklands. From the sturdy oak to the prickly holly, the foliage of these iconic trees exudes a timelessness that adds a touch of natural beauty to any setting, indoors or out.

YIELD: AT LEAST 6 FEET OF GARLAND

MATERIALS

Fresh Foliage (20 stems)
Fresh foliage is the main component of the garland, providing greenery and structure. Choose foliage from trees commonly found in Regency parklands, such as oak, beech, holly, or laurel, to capture the authentic look and feel of the era.

Garden Shears

Pruning shears are used to cut fresh foliage from trees. They ensure clean and precise cuts, allowing you to gather the foliage without damaging the trees.

Floral Wire or Twine (22 gauge, typically found in a 100-foot roll)

This is used to bind the foliage together and create the garland. Wire or twine provides support and structure, allowing you to shape the garland as desired.

Wire Cutters or Scissors

If you're using floral wire to bind the foliage together, wire cutters may be needed to trim the wire to the desired length. If you're using twine, scissors will do.

Decorative Accents (optional)

Decorative accents, such as ribbon, pine cones, or dried flowers, are optional additions to the garland that can add visual interest and personal flair.

INSTRUCTIONS

1. **Gather Foliage**

   Using your garden shears, cut and gather fresh foliage from your yard or garden.

2. **Prepare Foliage**

   Back at your workspace, use your shears to trim the branches to the desired length, removing any excess foliage or stems. Arrange the foliage in piles based on type or size to make it easier to work with.

3. **Create Base**

   Use floral wire as the base for your garland. Bend the wire into a desired shape or length to serve as the foundation for the garland.

4. **Arrange Foliage**

    Begin layering the foliage onto the base, starting with larger branches or leaves at the bottom and gradually adding smaller pieces on top. Experiment with different arrangements and combinations to achieve a balanced and visually appealing design.

5. **Secure Foliage**

    Use floral wire or twine to secure the foliage to the base, wrapping it tightly around the stems or branches at regular intervals along the length of the base. Ensure that the foliage is securely attached to prevent it from shifting or falling off.

6. **Add Decorative Accents (optional)**

    Enhance the beauty of your garland by adding decorative accents, such as ribbon, pine cones, or dried flowers. Attach these embellishments to the garland using floral wire, spacing them evenly throughout for a cohesive look.

7. **Hang and Enjoy**

    Once complete, hang your garland above a fire-place mantel, along a staircase railing, or across a doorway.

Acacia

ROBINIA PSEUDOACACIA

COMMON NAMES: BLACK LOCUST, FALSE ACACIA, BLACK LAUREL

SENSE AND SENSIBILITY

"**Acacia**" trees surround Cleveland and appear in the text as Elinor and Marianne journey through Somerset to the estate:

> *Cleveland was a spacious, modern-built house, situated on a sloping lawn. It had
> no park, but the pleasure-grounds were tolerably extensive; and like every other
> place of the same degree of importance, it had its open shrubbery, and closer*

*wood walk, a road of smooth gravel winding round a plantation, led to the front, the lawn was dotted over with timber, the house itself was under the guardianship of the fir, the mountain-ash, and the **acacia**, and a thick screen of them altogether, interspersed with tall Lombardy poplars, shut out the offices.*

While Jane references this tree as an "acacia," it is, in fact, the *R. pseudoacacia*, which is now commonly known as the black locust or false acacia.

The black locust is identified by its dark blue-green leaves with a lighter shade on the underside. In early summer, the tree produces large, fragrant clusters of flowers similar to orange blossoms. Unlike its doppelgänger, the honey locust, the black locust produces most of its spines on its sucker growth—offspring saplings that pop up near the parent tree.

A SHORT HISTORY OF BLACK LOCUST TREES

Black locusts, commonly but mistakenly called acacias, originated in the Americas and made their debut in England during the seventeenth century. By the 1700s and 1800s, the species had firmly established itself across the Atlantic, becoming a common presence in landscapes throughout England.

Renowned for its beauty, the black locust climbed to a high status during the Regency era, captivating gardeners with its distinctive appearance and clusters of white, fragrant flowers. Its popularity soared, making it a favored choice for ornamental planting.

Despite its American origins, the black locust has seamlessly integrated itself into English and European landscapes. Particularly prevalent in the south of England and along the east coast, it stands as a testament to its adaptability and resilience.

However, the black locust's unchecked proliferation has raised concerns in some regions, prompting efforts to regulate its spread due to its invasive nature. While certain areas in Europe and North America track and manage its pervasive presence, England lacks similar oversight, allowing the black locust to thrive.

The name "black locust" likely stems from its dark, deeply furrowed bark, which provides a stark contrast to the tree's vibrant foliage and delicate flowers, further adding to its mystique.

Apricot

PRUNUS ARMENIACA

COMMON NAMES: APRICOT, ARMENEAN PLUM, ANSU APRICOT

Apricots spread across the continents by way of China and the Silk Road. The fruit has smooth, velvety skin and tender flesh, which many people associate with summer. Like other stone fruit, apricots are versatile and can be eaten fresh, preserved, or baked into pastries.

The Moorpark apricot tree is known for its quick bloom time and can be expected to produce fruit within a year of planting. Typically, the tree also gives multiple flushes of fruit during a season, from midsummer to early fall. A smaller variety of apricot tree, it matures at a height of fifteen to twenty feet. The fruit is without fuzz, has deep-yellow skin, has flesh the color of orange or red-blush, and has a plumlike taste; it's considered one of the best apricot varieties.

MANSFIELD PARK

Jane specifically identifies the apricot tree in *Mansfield Park* as the Moorpark variety. Dr. Grant and Mrs. Norris argue about the tree's fruit and the factors contributing to its taste:

> *"It was only the spring twelvemonth before Mr. Norris's death that we put in the **apricot** against the stable wall, which is now grown such a noble tree, and getting to such perfection, sir," addressing herself then to Dr. Grant.*

> *"The tree thrives well, beyond a doubt, madam," replied Dr. Grant. "The soil is good; and I never pass it without regretting that the fruit should be so little worth the trouble of gathering."*

> *"Sir, it is a Moor Park, we bought it as a Moor Park, and it cost us—that is, it was a present from Sir Thomas, but I saw the bill—and I know it cost seven shillings, and was charged as a Moor Park."*

> *"You were imposed on, ma'am," replied Dr. Grant: "these potatoes have as much the flavour of a Moor Park **apricot** as the fruit from that tree. It is an insipid fruit at the best; but a good apricot is eatable, which none from my garden are."*

> *"The truth is, ma'am," said Mrs. Grant, pretending to whisper across the table to Mrs. Norris, "that Dr. Grant hardly knows what the natural taste of our **apricot** is: he is scarcely ever indulged with one, for it is so valuable a fruit; with a little assistance, and ours is such a remarkably large, fair sort, that what with early tarts and preserves, my cook contrives to get them all."*

A SHORT HISTORY OF APRICOT TREES

In 1542, Henry VIII's gardener brought apricots to England, but it wasn't until the 1760s that Lord Anson first planted the Moorpark variety on English soil at Moor Park in Hertfordshire. It quickly became a favorite and was rapidly grown, traded, and sold all over Europe.

During the Georgian era, apricots were a prized food item, often grown in walled gardens or greenhouses to protect them from the harsh English climate. While growing the trees in damp weather tended to be a struggle, innovations in garden and greenhouse design helped improve the trees' growth and fruit yield. The fruits were used in preserves, marmalades, and baked good, like cakes and tarts. Apricots were also dried and kept throughout the year.

Apricots were a well-loved fruit during the Regency, and their presence on a table or at a picnic was seen as a sign of wealth and status. Growing apricots was considered a mark of horticultural sophistication and technical mastery. In other words, if you could afford gardeners who could grow apricots, you were really living in style.

Today, the trees are still used by hobby gardeners. Aside from their deliciousness, apricots are rich in dietary fiber and contain many vitamins and minerals. Fresh apricots are available throughout the summer, while the preserved fruit can be purchased at the market year-round.

Cherry

PRUNUS SUBG. CERASUS

COMMON NAMES: *PRUNUS CERASUS*—SOUR CHERRY, TART CHERRY, DWARF CHERRY

PRUNUS AVIUM—SWEET CHERRY, WILD CHERRY, BIRD CHERRY, GEAN

Prunus avium, also known as the sweet **cherry** or wild cherry, is a medium-sized tree with a lifespan up to 150 years. In the spring, the sweet cherry produces white cup-shaped flowers that hang in clusters. Once pollinated, the flowers produce fruit that changes from a light shade of yellow or orange to deep red when ripe.

EMMA

The cherry is briefly mentioned in *Emma* after Mrs. Elton has had to bend over far too much to harvest strawberries, another sought-after fruit of the time. "Strawberries," she concludes, are "inferior to **cherries**." (See page 55 for the complete excerpt.)

It is possible that Jane was referencing either the sour cherry (*Prunus cerasus)* or the sweet cherry (*Prunus avium)*, but it is most likely she meant the latter, which was common during the Regency.

A SHORT HISTORY OF CHERRY TREES

The sweet cherry is native to western Asia and Europe but has been spread to other regions by migrating birds who transported its seeds in their droppings. The ancient Greeks and Romans were highly skilled at growing, grafting, and producing fruit trees, so it's no surprise that they cultivated many varieties of the fruit.

Eventually, cherries became a royal favorite, especially for Henry VIII. As the years went on, cherry trees became fixtures in orchards all over England. The earlier cherries were undoubtedly the sour variety, but as the years carried on, sweet cherries became a more fashionable choice. During the Georgian era, cherries were a delicacy. They could be eaten raw, used to make preserves, or added to baked goods, like biscuits, cakes, and tarts. Cherry juice was also a common Regency treat. When not consumed, it was used instead of makeup to stain the cheeks and lips.

In the garden, the cherry, with its gorgeous pink or white flowers, was sought after as a focal tree. It was often planted in parklands, public parks, and private formal gardens. Today, *Prunus avium* has hundreds of cultivars used in gardening and landscape design. Some cultivars are more ornamental, while others are bred to produce crops of fruit. Still others are grown for their wood, which is used to make furniture and smoke foods.

Chestnut

CASTANEA SATIVA

COMMON NAMES: SPANISH CHESTNUT, SWEET CHESTNUT, EUROPEAN CHESTNUT

The Spanish **chestnut** is a true behemoth of a tree that can live up to seven hundred years. One of its most noted features is the diameter of its trunk, which, at full maturity, can reach seven feet. In landscape design, the trees are planted for their ample shade and impressive height. Many Spanish chestnuts stretch over one hundred feet tall.

When the Spanish chestnut flowers, it produces long yellow blooms. The chestnut fruit is edible and is often roasted and eaten as a festive snack or used in recipes for stuffing and cakes.

PRIDE AND PREJUDICE

The Spanish chestnut and the oak are mentioned in *Pride and Prejudice* during Elizabeth's visit to see Miss Darcy at Pemberley:

> *On reaching the house, they were shown through the hall into the saloon, whose northern aspect rendered it delightful for the summer. Its windows opening to the ground, admitted a most refreshing view of the high woody hills behind the house, and of the beautiful oaks and **Spanish chestnuts** which were scattered over the intermediate lawn.*

A SHORT HISTORY OF CHESTNUT TREES

The Spanish chestnut, also known as the sweet chestnut, was introduced to England through the Romans' influence. It joined myriad other foreign species introduced to the island during the Roman occupation.

During the Georgian era, chestnut trees played a pivotal role in enhancing the visual appeal of gardens. They boasted splendid foliage, striking blooms, and distinctive, spiny husks. Their substantial size made them favored as focal points in parklands and gardens, and they also provided ample shade to escape the summer heat.

Today, Spanish chestnuts continue to hold significance both as a valuable food crop and for landscaping purposes. However, confusion often arises between Spanish chestnuts and horse chestnuts, as their nuts have similarities but their leaves differ significantly. Horse chestnuts feature hand-shaped leaves, whereas Spanish chestnuts are characterized by long toothed leaves.

Fir

ABIES ALBA

COMMON NAMES: SILVER FIR, EUROPEAN SILVER FIR, COMMON SILVER FIR

The European silver **fir** is a conifer native to the mountains of Europe, from the Balkans to the Pyrenees. While it is often confused with the spruce and Douglas fir, it can be identified by the length and color of its needles and by its cones, which appear high in the tree and stand upright (unlike spruce and Douglas fir cones, which dangle). The cones will break and disperse the seeds while still attached to a branch.

JANE AUSTEN, HER LIFE AND LETTERS: A FAMILY RECORD

In November 1800, Jane Austen wrote to her sister, Cassandra, lamenting the destruction caused by a violent storm that ravaged some of her beloved trees at Steventon, the family's rectory in Hampshire—a personal loss that deeply affected her:

> *We have had a dreadful storm of wind in the fore part of this day, which has done a great deal of mischief among our trees. I was sitting alone in the dining-room when an odd kind of crash startled me—in a moment afterwards it was repeated; descend into the Sweep!!!!! The other, which had fallen, I suppose, in the first crash, and which was the nearest to the pond, taking a more easterly direction, sunk among our screen of chestnuts and **firs**, knocking down one spruce-**fir**, beating off the head of another, and stripping the two corner chestnuts of several branches in its fall.*

A SHORT HISTORY OF FIR TREES

The term "fir" today refers specifically to a certain type of coniferous tree, but during the Georgian era, it was a more general term encompassing all conifers. Despite their broad usage in English landscapes, none of the roughly fifty species of fir trees worldwide are native to England. The silver fir, however, found its way to the island in 1603 and swiftly naturalized. Now thriving in the wild, it has become a familiar sight.

Distinguished by its impressive size, shimmering color, and varied texture, the silver fir became a sought-after addition to parks and estate gardens during the Georgian era. Its presence added vertical interest and depth to garden designs of the time, drawing the gaze upwards and enhancing the visual appeal of landscapes.

Even today, the silver fir continues to flourish across England, particularly in the woodlands of the northwest. Its wood, prized for its resistance to moisture and durability, remains highly sought after for various applications, from sauna construction to window frames and outdoor structures. Silver fir wood stands as a testament to both its natural beauty and its practical utility, perpetuating its legacy as a valued component of England's natural landscape and architectural heritage.

Hazel

CORYLUS AVELLANA

COMMON NAMES: COMMON HAZEL, EUROPEAN HAZELNUT, EUROPEAN FILBERT,
EUROPEAN COBNUT

The common **hazel**, *Corylus avellana*, is a small tree that is sometimes categorized as a shrub. While hazel is usually coppiced, or cut back to ground level to force new growth, if the tree is left to mature, it can reach a height of twenty feet. Coppiced, nurtured hazel trees can live for hundreds of years.

Hazel flowers form as catkins that hang in clusters from the branches of the tree. The yellow flowers start to bloom before the start of spring. Once pollinated, the nuts take all spring and summer to mature and are typically ready for harvest by the beginning of fall.

PERSUASION

In *Persuasion*, Captain Wentworth plucks a hazelnut from a limb while walking down the center of a hedgerow with Louisa. He muses over the strength of the nut and how it has managed to hang on to the limb while others have fallen underfoot:

> *"Here is a nut," said he, catching one down from an upper bough, "to exemplify: a beautiful glossy nut, which, blessed with original strength, has outlived all the storms of autumn. Not a puncture, not a weak spot anywhere. This nut," he continued, with playful solemnity, "while so many of his brethren have fallen and been trodden under foot, is still in possession of all the happiness that a **hazel** nut can be supposed capable of."*

A SHORT HISTORY OF HAZEL TREES

The common hazel tree, native to England and Europe, northern Africa, and western Asia, boasts a rich history of versatile utility and cultural significance. Renowned for its pliable wood, hazel has been utilized for various purposes throughout the ages, from thatching roofs and crafting furniture to fashioning trapping implements and stakes for fishing nets. Its flexible nature has made it indispensable to many common crafts.

In the English countryside, copses of mature hazel trees are a common sight, reflecting the long-standing tradition of coppicing. Traditionally, hazel trees were typically coppiced on an eight-year cycle, ensuring a steady supply of timber for both practical and ornamental use.

During the Regency era, hazel trees found favor in informal garden and landscape designs, appreciated for their ability to form dense copses and contribute to the creation of naturalistic scenery. Their presence added depth and character to the English countryside, blending seamlessly with other native species, like oak and birch, in woodlands, hedgerows, and parklands.

Today, hazel trees continue to thrive worldwide, their adaptability allowing them to flourish in diverse environments. In England, they remain integral to the landscape, serving as enduring reminders of their cultural and ecological significance.

Holly

ILEX AQUIFOLIUM

COMMON NAMES: COMMON HOLLY, ENGLISH HOLLY

Holly, *Ilex aquifolium*, is an evergreen tree sometimes classified as a shrub. If left to grow to full height, it can reach fifty feet tall. Its spiny leaves are a glossy dark green on the top side and light green on the underside.

In the middle of spring, the white holly flower begins to open. Once pollinated, its "berries"—which are actually drupes, or stone fruits—begin to form. The drupes stay green until the fall, when they turn the characteristic bright shade of red.

PERSUASION

Holly is mentioned in *Persuasion* when Louisa is eavesdropping on Anne and Captain Wentworth in the hedgerow. Louisa hides from the pair by sneaking behind a prickly shrub of holly:

> *For herself—she feared to move, lest she should be seen. While she remained, a bush of low rambling **holly** protected her, and they were moving on.*

A SHORT HISTORY OF HOLLY TREES

Holly, native to the British Isles, Europe, western Asia, and northern Africa, stands as one of England's most ubiquitous evergreens, gracing gardens, woodlands, and parklands for centuries. Throughout its storied history, holly has been esteemed for its distinctive dark-green foliage and vibrant red drupes, making it a favored ornamental shrub during the Georgian era. Its adaptability to diverse soil conditions further contributed to its popularity as a decorative feature in landscapes of all types.

Amid England's industrial transformation from the mid- to late 1800s, holly gained newfound recognition for its remarkable resilience to urbanization and pollution. Thriving even in heavily populated and polluted industrial areas, such as London, holly emerged as a symbol of nature's enduring strength and vitality amid the changing urban landscape.

Today, holly continues to flourish in the wilds of England, adorning woodlands and hedgerows with its timeless beauty. It remains a cherished presence in centuries-old established gardens, where classic varieties retain their appeal alongside a rich tapestry of cultivated plants. With more than two hundred cultivars boasting differences in size, leaf shape, and berry color, holly offers a wealth of options for contemporary gardeners and enthusiasts. From traditional varieties with red drupes to unique cultivars producing yellow drupes, holly continues to captivate with its ever-evolving diversity and enduring charm.

Larch

LARIX DECIDUA

COMMON NAME: EUROPEAN LARCH, COMMON LARCH

The European **larch**, *Larix decidua*, is a tall-growing conifer in the pine family. It's the only deciduous coniferous tree in the United Kingdom, shedding all its needles in the winter. In fact, it's the only member of the Pinaceae family to do this: when fall comes, the needles turn a glorious shade of gold and fall to the ground in a thick mat, only to be regrown in the springtime.

MANSFIELD PARK

Larch grows alongside laurel and beech trees in the wilderness of Sotherton and is mentioned as the Crawfords, Fanny, and Edmund make their way across the lawn toward the terrace and the wilderness:

> *A considerable flight of steps landed them in the wilderness, which was a planted wood of about two acres, and though chiefly of **larch** and laurel, and beech cut down, and though laid out with too much regularity, was darkness and shade, and natural beauty, compared with the bowling-green and the terrace. They all felt the refreshment of it, and for some time could only walk and admire.*

A SHORT HISTORY OF LARCH TREES

The European larch, originally hailing from the alpine regions of central Europe—such as Austria, Germany, and Switzerland—found its way to England in the early 1600s. Beyond its practical use, the larch emerged as a prominent feature in Georgian landscape design, prized for its imposing stature and needlelike foliage, which added texture and visual interest to gardens.

Today, the European larch remains a familiar sight in parks and gardens throughout England. It thrives in forests and woodlands, where its towering presence provides shelter for wildlife, including squirrels, birds, and insects.

However, the species faces a significant threat from *Phytophthora ramorum*, a fungus-like pathogen transmitted via airborne spores. Once infected, larch trees cannot be cured. The only way to stop an infestation is to cut down infected trees as soon as the fungus is spotted. While the prevalence of the pathogen poses a serious challenge to larch tree populations, concerted efforts in disease management and research may mitigate the risk of extinction.

Laurel

PRUNUS LAUROCERASUS

COMMON NAMES: CHERRY LAUREL, COMMON LAUREL, ENGLISH LAUREL,

VERSAILLES LAUREL

The cherry **laurel** is not a true laurel at all. The true laurels, which belong to the Lauracaea family, are known more for their culinary uses than for creating a hedge in a garden. The cherry laurel is part of the *Prunus*, or cherry, genus. Its common name comes from the leaf's resemblance to true laurel species and the fruit the plant produces. It's also often called the common laurel and the Versailles laurel.

In the spring, the cherry laurel produces small white flowers. The fruits—which are technically drupes, like those of the wild cherry and holly—turn from a vibrant red to almost black as they mature into the fall.

PRIDE AND PREJUDICE

In *Pride and Prejudice,* a hedge of laurel surrounds the Collins's parsonage:

> *At length the Parsonage was discernible. The garden sloping to the road, the house standing in it, the green pales, and the **laurel** hedge, everything declared they were arriving.*

MANSFIELD PARK

In *Mansfield Park,* laurel is one of the trees, together with larch and beech, that surround Sotherton. (See page 112 for the complete excerpt.)

Later on in the novel, Fanny praises the laurel:

> *"I am so glad to see the evergreens thrive!" said Fanny, in reply. "My uncle's gardener always says the soil here is better than his own, and so it appears from the growth of the **laurels** and evergreens in general."*

EMMA

In *Emma,* Mrs. Elton compares the laurels growing at Hartfield to those that grow at Maple Grove:

> *"The **laurels** at Maple Grove are in the same profusion as here, and stand very much in the same way—just across the lawn; and I had a glimpse of a fine large tree, with a bench round it, which put me so exactly in mind!"*

It's most likely that Jane was referring to *Prunus laurocerasus* because the plant was used in England at the beginning of the nineteenth century. A look-alike called the Portuguese laurel, or *Prunus lusitanica,* didn't become prominent until later.

A SHORT HISTORY OF LAUREL TREES

The cherry laurel is native to southeastern Europe and parts of western Asia along the Black Sea. It was introduced to England in the sixteenth century, and, like many other plants introduced by explorers, it jumped ship and escaped the bounds of controlled garden design. It was first found in the wild in England in 1886 and is now considered a naturalized species.

In Georgian garden design, the cherry laurel was an ornamental shrub often planted in rows or clusters to create a privacy screen or boundary fence. Its dense foliage also made it useful for blocking wind or containing livestock.

Cherry laurel is now considered invasive in many regions, including England, because it competes with and pushes out true native species. Despite this classification, the shrub is still widely used in garden and landscape design, often as a hedge, boundary screen, or privacy fence.

Lime

TILIA × EUROPAEA

COMMON NAMES: LINDEN TREE, EUROPEAN LIME, COMMON LIME

Though unrelated to the citrus fruit, **linden trees** are often called **"limes"** in England. This nomenclature likely stems from a linguistic association with the word "linden," rooted in terms meaning "flexible" or "to flex."

A popular ornamental tree in English gardens and parks, the common lime, *Tilia × europaea*, is a hybrid with characteristics of both its parents: the large-leaved and small-leaved lime trees. It grows rapidly—roughly fifteen to twenty-four inches a year if the growing conditions are right—and can reach heights of seventy feet or above. The leaves, flowers, and fruit of the linden are edible and are frequently used in teas, syrups, and sauces and as a thickening agent.

These trees thrive on the seasons and need a hot summer to flower. However, the common lime trees can sprout from fallen branches, so if a few years go by without a hot summer, these trees will reproduce anyway.

EMMA

Lime trees are mentioned in *Emma* during the scene at Donwell Abbey. Emma and company take a stroll around the abbey's pleasure grounds. They are led down a path of limes to a view of the river:

> It was hot; and after walking some time over the gardens in a scattered, dispersed way, scarcely any three together, they insensibly followed one another to the delicious shade of a broad short avenue of **limes**, which stretching beyond the garden at an equal distance from the river, seemed the finish of the pleasure grounds.—It led to nothing: nothing but a view at the end over a low stone wall with high pillars, which seemed intended, in their erection, to give the appearance of an approach to the house, which never had been there.

A SHORT HISTORY OF LIME TREES

The common lime, native to England and closely associated with its parent trees' habitats, has been widely cultivated throughout the region, gracing various landscapes, from parks and estates to churchyards and avenues.

The inherent flexibility of the lime tree played a pivotal role in its utilization in landscape design. Often planted in rows and trained to create living tunnels through a weaving technique known as pleaching, lime trees became iconic features in Georgian gardens, adorning avenues and serving as focal points in expansive parkland landscapes.

Even today, the common lime remains highly valued for its shade-providing canopy and the resilience of its wood. Renowned for its robust nature and ability to thrive in diverse soil conditions, the lime tree continues to serve as a vital habitat for various wildlife species, from caterpillars to birds, bees, and ants.

Given its substantial size upon reaching maturity, the common lime is an ideal choice for open spaces, while its rapid growth and positive response to pruning make it a preferred option for hedging purposes. As a versatile and enduring component of England's natural and cultivated landscapes, the common lime endures as a symbol of resilience and vitality, enriching its surroundings with its graceful presence.

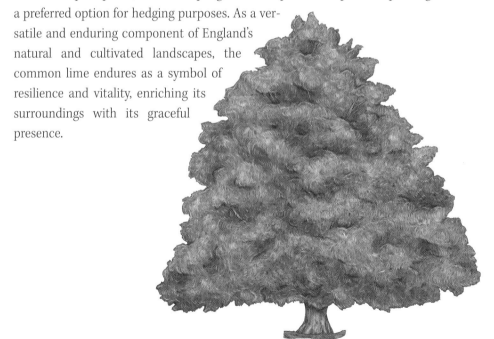

Lombardy Poplar

POPULUS NIGRA ITALICA

COMMON NAMES: LOMBARDY POPLAR

The **Lombardy poplar** is a fast-growing deciduous tree known for its distinctive columnar shape. Reaching heights of up to one hundred feet, it is often planted in rows to create windbreaks or to line streets and driveways. The tree has a relatively short lifespan of around fifty years, though some can live longer under ideal conditions.

The tree is prized for its rapid growth, which can exceed six feet per year, making it an excellent choice for quick landscape impact.

This tree prefers full sun and well-drained soil but is adaptable to various soil types. However, it is susceptible to several diseases that can shorten its lifespan.

SENSE AND SENSIBILITY

Lombardy poplars are mentioned in *Sense and Sensibility* in the description of the Palmers' estate. A screen of fir, mountain ash, and acacia "interspersed with tall Lombardy poplars" surrounds the property. (See page 96 for the complete excerpt.)

A SHORT HISTORY OF LOMBARDY POPLAR TREES

The Lombardy poplar is a naturally occurring mutation of the black poplar. Early records indicate it was first seen in Italy at the start of the eighteenth century. Botanists realized it could easily be propagated from cuttings of the male tree, and those saplings were shipped all over Europe to be studied. Identifiable by its shape but sometimes confused for the black poplar, the Lombardy poplar is a narrow deciduous tree that can reach a height of sixty feet. However, it typically dies from disease within its first twenty years.

In England, the Lombardy poplar quickly became a staple in landscape and garden design, remaining popular throughout the Georgian era. Its rapid growth and tall, slender profile made it ideal for avenues and windbreaks and was often used as a striking accent tree in formal gardens, providing contrast with rounder trees.

Today, Lombardy poplars line boulevards, lanes, and property boundaries worldwide. Many gardeners—both hobbyists and professionals—are unaware of their drawbacks and plant them for their aesthetic appeal. These trees, especially problematic in regions with sticky clay soil, like England, often cause damage to nearby buildings, sidewalks, and roads due to their invasive root systems.

Mountain Ash

SORBUS AUCUPARIA

COMMON NAMES: EUROPEAN MOUNTAIN ASH, ROWAN

The **mountain ash** can grow up to fifty feet tall and live for two hundred years or more.

It is native to England as well as most of Europe and northern Asia. Commonly found in the wild at high altitudes, the tree is named for its love of mountain climes and similarity to the true ash tree, *Fraxinus*, for which it is often confused.

SENSE AND SENSIBILITY

Mountain ash, contemporarily known in England as the rowan, is mentioned in *Sense and Sensibility* as one of the trees, along with fir and acacia, surrounding Cleveland.

The house is described as "under the guardianship" of those trees and surrounded by a "thick screen" of them interspersed with Lombardy poplars. (See page 96 for the complete excerpt.)

JANE AUSTEN, HER LIFE AND LETTERS: A FAMILY RECORD

In October 1800, Jane penned a letter to her sister, Cassandra, detailing the alterations being made to the grounds at Steventon, the family's rectory in Hampshire:

> *Our improvements have advanced very well; the bank along the elm walk is sloped down for the reception of thorns and lilacs, and it is settled that the other side of the path is to continue turfed, and to be planted with beech, **ash**, and larch.*

A SHORT HISTORY OF MOUNTAIN ASH TREES

In Georgian landscape design, the European mountain ash served multiple purposes, contributing to the creation of diverse groves, natural fences, or privacy screens. Its vibrant red berries and delicate foliage rendered it a popular choice for ornamental planting in gardens, adding both beauty and functionality.

Over time, this tree's versatility and cultural significance have solidified its place in gardening practices and traditions, leaving a lasting impact on English horticulture. Today, the mountain ash can be spotted adorning city avenues, tucked into garden corners, or thriving in the wild. The ongoing growth of modern cultivars has further enhanced its appeal, with breeders selecting for specific visual attributes such as fruit color, leaf shape, and branch structure.

Mulberry

MORUS NIGRA

COMMON NAME: BLACK MULBERRY

The black **mulberry** is a deciduous tree that is famous and sought after for its fruit. It's a slow-growing species with a dense, sprawling crown of branches. In the late spring, the tree produces catkins that, once pollinated, bear dark, oblong fruit.

The fruit is delicious and highly prized because it is typically unavailable on the commercial market. At the harvesting stage, around the end of August, the fruit of the black mulberry is too soft to transport long distances because it is damaged easily. It's best used or consumed within a day of picking.

SENSE AND SENSIBILITY

In *Sense and Sensibility*, Mrs. Jennings enthusiastically describes the beauties of Colonel Brandon's estate, including its mulberry tree, as she tries to persuade others of the merits of a potential match between Colonel Brandon and Marianne.

*"Delaford is a nice place, I can tell you; exactly what I call a nice old fashioned place, full of comforts and conveniences; quite shut in with great garden walls that are covered with the best fruit-trees in the country; and such a **mulberry** tree in one corner!"*

THE LETTERS OF JANE AUSTEN: THE BRABOURNE EDITION

In May 1811, Jane wrote to her sister, Cassandra, and shared news of life in Chawton with her unmistakable wit:

*"I will not say that your **mulberry-trees** are dead, but I am afraid they are not alive."*

A SHORT HISTORY OF MULBERRY TREES

The introduction of the black mulberry tree to England has sparked a long-standing debate over its origins. While many attribute its arrival to James I's efforts to bolster the silk industry, silkworms prefer the leaves of the white mulberry over the black mulberry and were unable to truly thrive. However, evidence suggests that the black mulberry had already taken root in England centuries before James I's reign. Archaeological excavations near the Thames revealed black mulberry seeds in Roman settlements dating back to the first century, indicating their presence in London long before James I's time.

The medieval period saw the deliberate cultivation of mulberry trees in infirmary gardens of monasteries and abbeys, but this practice was disrupted by the dissolution of monasteries under Henry VIII. Despite this setback, mulberries remained popular in Georgian England, admired for their ornamental value in formal gardens and their versatile fruit, used in various culinary delights of the era.

Today, mulberry trees are ubiquitous in modern England, often found in unexpected locations, such as hedgerows and churchyards, and tended to by local enthusiasts. The Morus Londinium project aims to document the history of surviving mulberry trees in London, with the oldest known specimen dating back to 1548 in Syon Park.

Myrtle

MYRTUS COMMUNIS

COMMON NAMES: COMMON MYRTLE, FOXTAIL MYRTLE, SWEET MYRTLE

The common **myrtle**, *Myrtus communis,* is a medium-sized upright shrub that produces flowers in late spring. After pollination, the blooms produce dark-purple berries. Many gardeners prune myrtle to keep it as a topiary or bonsai, but others prefer the plant in its shrubbier form. Myrtle can also be trained as a low-mounding shrub or a completely upright tree.

MANSFIELD PARK

In *Mansfield Park*, Mary, Mrs. Grant, Fanny, and Edmund discuss the state of Mrs. Grant's garden, the impending cold weather, and the threat of a freeze. Mary mentions that, with enough money, one can even buy myrtle, highlighting the potential for myrtle to be sold for profit:

> *"Thank you; but there is no escaping these little vexations, Mary, live where we may; and when you are settled in town and I come to see you, I dare say I shall find you with yours, in spite of the nurseryman and the poulterer, perhaps on their very account. Their remoteness and unpunctuality, or their exorbitant charges and frauds, will be drawing forth bitter lamentations."*

> *"I mean to be too rich to lament or to feel anything of the sort. A large income is the best recipe for happiness I ever heard of. It certainly may secure all the **myrtle** and turkey part of it."*

> *"You intend to be very rich?" said Edmund, with a look which, to Fanny's eye, had a great deal of serious meaning.*

> *"To be sure. Do not you? Do not we all?"*

A SHORT HISTORY OF MYRTLE TREES

Originally from the Middle East, *Myrtus communis* has been cultivated in England since the sixteenth century. During the Middle Ages, it was highly regarded for its medicinal properties, believed to possess cleansing and purifying qualities, and was utilized in the creation of perfumes and tinctures. Symbolizing love and marriage, myrtle is a prominent feature in wedding ceremonies and celebrations, often incorporated into bridal wreaths to signify the bride's happiness and fidelity.

By the nineteenth century, myrtle became a popular choice in horticultural design, utilized as a hedge plant and in topiaries by Regency garden designers. Today, it is commonly grown both in landscapes and containers, particularly favored for its ability to thrive in warm climates, making container planting a practical option for indoor winter protection.

Various parts of the myrtle plant, including its fruits, flowers, and leaves, offer culinary applications. Whether dried or used fresh, they impart herbal flavors to dishes and baked goods.

Oak

QUERCUS ROBUR

COMMON NAME: ENGLISH OAK, COMMON OAK

The English **oak** is a very large deciduous tree that, at full maturity, can reach over 130 feet tall. It's known for its large crown and wide breadth, which create ample shade.

Oaks produce acorns that first appear tiny and green in the summer and ripen to dark brown in the fall. The nut falls from the canopy to germinate and sprout the following spring.

MANSFIELD PARK

In *Mansfield Park*, Mr. Rushworth plans to remove an avenue of oak trees at Sotherton:

"Now, where is the avenue? The house fronts the east, I perceive. The avenue, there-fore, must be at the back of it. Mr. Rushworth talked of the west front."

*"Yes, it is exactly behind the house; begins at a little distance, and ascends for half a mile to the extremity of the grounds. You may see something of it here—something of the more distant trees. It is **oak** entirely."*

Fanny later sought shelter there when she got caught in a sudden rainstorm near the parsonage:

*Fanny, having been sent into the village on some errand by her aunt Norris, was overtaken by a heavy shower close to the Parsonage; and being descried from one of the windows endeavouring to find shelter under the branches and lingering leaves of an **oak** just beyond their premises, was forced, though not without some modest reluctance on her part, to come in.*

NORTHANGER ABBEY

Oak dots the landscape in *Northanger Abbey*. The very chatty Henry mentions the oak on the group's walk to Beechen Cliff:

*Delighted with her progress, and fearful of wearying her with too much wisdom at once, Henry suffered the subject to decline, and by an easy transition from a piece of rocky fragment and the withered **oak** which he had placed near its summit, to **oaks** in general, to forests, the enclosure of them, waste lands, crown lands and government, he shortly found himself arrived at politics; and from politics, it was an easy step to silence.*

Later, Catherine learns that tall oak trees surround the entire estate of Northanger Abbey:

Many were the inquiries she was eager to make of Miss Tilney; but so active were her thoughts, that when these inquiries were answered, she was hardly more assured than before, of Northanger Abbey having been a richly endowed convent at the time of the Reformation, of its having fallen into the hands of an ancestor *of the Tilneys on its dissolution, of a large portion of the ancient building still making a part of the present dwelling although the rest was decayed, or of its standing low in a valley, sheltered from the north and east by rising woods of **oak**.*

Then, the same ancient oaks are mentioned as Catherine describes Northanger as a gothic setting:

*As they drew near the end of their journey, her impatience for a sight of the abbey—for some time suspended by his conversation on subjects very different— returned in full force, and every bend in the road was expected with solemn awe to afford a glimpse of its massy walls of grey stone, rising amidst a grove of ancient **oaks**, with the last beams of the sun playing in beautiful splendour on its high Gothic windows. But so low did the building stand, that she found herself passing through the great gates of the lodge into the very grounds of Northanger, without having discerned even an antique chimney.*

But oak trees are more than landscape features at Northanger Abbey. Oak is also the wood that makes up the grand staircase of the abbey:

*Returning through the large and lofty hall, they ascended a broad staircase of shining **oak**, which, after many flights and many landing-places, brought them upon a long, wide gallery.*

PRIDE AND PREJUDICE

At Pemberley, "beautiful **oaks**" are present on the lawn, alongside the Spanish chestnuts. (See page 104 for the complete excerpt.)

A SHORT HISTORY OF OAK TREES

Oaks, revered for their grandeur and longevity, have long held a significant place in landscape design. Their majestic stature and enduring presence made them prized additions to prominent locations, where they were often allowed to grow naturally, their expansive canopies providing both shade and visual intrigue. Conversely, in formal garden settings, oaks were sometimes meticulously pruned and guided to form symmetrical avenues or alleys, showcasing their adaptability to various design styles.

Among the oak species native to England, *Quercus robur*, or the English oak, stands alongside *Quercus petraea*, the sessile oak. Given its prevalence during the Regency era and its significance in the English landscape, it is highly probable that Jane Austen's novels reference *Q. robur*.

Even today, the English oak remains a familiar sight in woodlands and fields throughout England, as its towering presence makes it an ideal choice for large gardens and open spaces. Despite its gigantic size, many gardeners delight in training the oak as a hedge, keeping it pruned to a manageable scale while still retaining its characteristic charm and character.

Pear

PYRUS COMMUNIS

COMMON NAME: EUROPEAN PEAR, COMMON PEAR

The European **pear** is a deciduous tree native to central and eastern Europe and southwest Asia. It grows up to thirty feet tall, with glossy green leaves and white flowers that bloom in early spring. The flowers, when pollinated, give way to fruit, which grows quickly on the tree and ripens from bright green to gold. The fruits are typically harvested in late summer. Popular cultivars include Bartlett, Bosc, and Anjou.

PERSUASION

Pear trees are mentioned in *Persuasion* in the description of the parsonage at Uppercross:

> *Uppercross was a moderate-sized village, which a few years back had been completely in the old English style, containing only two houses superior in appearance*

*to those of the yeomen and labourers; the mansion of the squire, with its high walls, great gates, and old trees, substantial and unmodernized, and the compact, tight parsonage, enclosed in its own neat garden, with a vine and a **pear-tree** trained round its casements . . .*

A SHORT HISTORY OF PEAR TREES

The pear tree has a rich history dating back to ancient times. Both the ancient Romans and Greeks cultivated it for its medicinal properties, and ultimately the Romans introduced the pear tree to England, where it thrived. By the fourteenth century, a prized variety called the black Worcester pear was being grown in and around the city of Worcester. It was so impressive that, in 1575, Queen Elizabeth I adopted it as a symbol of the city, further cementing its legacy.

By the end of the 1700s and into the Georgian era, new varieties of pears were being introduced from other European countries. The fruit was used for cooking, baking, and making perry, an alcoholic beverage made from fermented pears. Pear trees were also frequently used in garden design. Like apple, peach, and nectarine, pear trees were often espaliered against walls to maximize the space and to help encourage the tree to fruit. They were also used as ornamental elements in formal gardens and parks, or as part of a large design within a parkland landscape.

Today, the common naturalized pear can be found in English hedges, woodlands, and gardens. Pear trees tend to spread easily through dropped fruit, which explains how they have escaped cultivation and now grow wild across the country.

Scotch Pine

PINUS SYLVESTRIS

COMMON NAMES: SCOTS PINE, SCOTCH PINE, BALTIC PINE, SCOTS FIR

The **Scotch pine** or Scots pine is a venerable evergreen conifer native to northern Europe and Asia. This remarkable tree has been known to live for more than seven hundred years and reach heights of more than one hundred feet at maturity. Its pollinated flowers develop into green cones that take a full season to mature, resulting in a range of cone sizes on the tree at any given time. The mature cones are gray, with a distinctive bump on each scale.

NORTHANGER ABBEY

Jane references a "Scotch fir" and a pine forest tree in *Northanger Abbey*. During the Regency era, the Scotch pine was commonly called a "Scots fir" in many regions of England. Therefore, Jane was possibly referring to the Scots pine in both instances. However, because of the Alps and Pyrenees reference, it's difficult to tell.

Mrs. Tilney adores a walk lined with "Scotch firs" in *Northanger Abbey*:

*It was a narrow winding path through a thick grove of old **Scotch firs**; and Catherine, struck by its gloomy aspect, and eager to enter it, could not, even by the General's disapprobation, be kept from stepping forward.*

Catherine also mentions pines when she is musing over her gothic literature obsession:

*Charming as were all Mrs. Radcliffe's works, and charming even as were the works of all her imitators, it was not in them perhaps that human nature, at least in the Midland counties of England, was to be looked for. Of the Alps and Pyrenees, with their **pine forests** and their vices, they might give a faithful delineation; and Italy, Switzerland, and the south of France might be as fruitful in horrors as they were there represented. Catherine dared not doubt beyond her own country, and even of that, if hard pressed, would have yielded the northern and western extremities.*

A SHORT HISTORY OF SCOTCH PINE TREES

The Scots pine holds significance in England's history and landscape, as it is the only pine native to the isle. Throughout the centuries, Scots pine forests provided resources for construction, fuel, and other essential needs, contributing to the nation's economic and industrial development at the cost of rampant deforestation in the Highlands. During the Regency, landscape designers favored the Scots pine because of its towering stature and rustic charm. The trees were also valued as a timber resource for construction and naval use. England's expanding urban centers required timber for housing and infrastructure, while the Royal Navy relied on sturdy timber for shipbuilding.

Today, the Scots pine remains endangered, though through conservation efforts, it is making a comeback in its native habitat.

Spruce

PICEA ABIES

COMMON NAME: NORWAY SPRUCE, EUROPEAN SPRUCE

The Norway **spruce** is an evergreen conifer that, at over 130 feet tall, forms a towering triangular shape sought after in the picturesque tradition. It has a characteristic smell that many associate with the winter holidays.

EMMA

Although the spruce tree itself is not mentioned in *Emma*, a specific spruce byproduct is. Here, Harriet recalls how Mr. Knightley says that he brews spruce beer, which is made using the needles of the tree:

"This was really his," said Harriet.—"Do not you remember one morning?—no, I dare say you do not. But one morning—I forget exactly the day—but perhaps it was the Tuesday or Wednesday before that evening, *he wanted to make a memorandum in his pocket-book; it was about* **spruce***-beer. Mr. Knightley had been telling him something about brewing spruce-beer"* . . .

"I do remember it," cried Emma; "I perfectly remember it.—Talking about spruce-beer.—Oh! yes—Mr. Knightley and I both saying we liked it, and Mr. Elton's seeming resolved to learn to like it too."

While both the Norway spruce and black spruce (*Picea mariana*) were used to make beer throughout the nineteenth century, the prevalence of Norway spruce in England during Jane's lifetime suggests she would have had it in mind while writing *Emma*.

A SHORT HISTORY OF NORWAY SPRUCE TREES

During the nineteenth century, the Norway spruce was planted in a blanket fashion all over England to supplement the native timber in the forests—but one of the most prevalent historical uses of the spruce was undoubtedly as the Christmas tree. In 1840, Prince Albert, the husband of Queen Victoria, introduced the old German custom of decorating a spruce tree with lit candles for Christmas. (Although Queen Charlotte had decorated a yew tree for Christmas forty years prior, Prince Albert is generally credited with popularizing the tradition in England.) Over time, the Norway spruce became the fashionable choice for Christmas trees across both Europe and the United Kingdom. To this day, a massive Norway spruce is felled and shipped to London from Norway each year to be displayed in Trafalgar Square throughout the holiday season.

And in the Georgian era, before it was decorated at Yuletide in England, the Norway spruce was used to make spruce beer—a fermented beverage made by boiling the tips or young shoots of the tree with water, sugar, and other spices.

Today, as a holiday staple, the Norway spruce plays a vital role in woodland conservation. It is strategically planted to offer food and shelter to red squirrels, whose population has dwindled in England due to increased environmental temperature and long periods of drought.

Walnut

JUGLANS REGIA

COMMON NAMES: ENGLISH WALNUT, COMMON WALNUT,

PERSIAN WALNUT, MADEIRA WALNUT

The **walnut** tree is a broadleaf deciduous tree that can grow to over one hundred feet tall. As opposed to tall oak trees, the walnut is a short-trunked tree. The male flowers of the walnut appear as long neon-green catkins. After pollination, the female flowers become dense husks that encase the walnuts.

SENSE AND SENSIBILITY

In *Sense and Sensibility*, Elinor and Marianne's half-brother, John Dashwood, has made plans to cut down the walnut trees behind the women's childhood home to make space to build a greenhouse for his wife, Fanny:

> *"Another year or two may do much towards it," [John] gravely replied; "but however there is still a great deal to be done. There is not a stone laid of Fanny's green-house, and nothing but the plan of the flower-garden marked out."*
>
> *"Where is the green-house to be?"*
>
> *"Upon the knoll behind the house. The old **walnut** trees are all come down to make room for it. It will be a very fine object from many parts of the park, and the flower-garden will slope down just before it, and be exceedingly pretty. We have cleared away all the old thorns that grew in patches over the brow."*

Elinor kept her concern and her censure to herself; and was very thankful that Marianne was not present, to share the provocation.

Elinor is forced to keep her feelings to herself, but she is clearly quite vexed with her brother. This is one of several instances of Jane villainizing a character through the felling of trees.

A SHORT HISTORY OF WALNUT TREES

The walnut tree, native to regions spanning from southeast Europe to southwest China, has left an indelible mark on England's landscape and cultural heritage. Believed to have been introduced by the Romans, who recognized the value of its nuts and timber, the walnut became a cherished and cultivated species in English gardens for centuries. Its ornamental beauty further enhanced its appeal, making it a favored choice in landscape design.

However, its significance transcended mere aesthetic appeal; throughout history, various parts of the walnut tree were utilized for medicinal, practical, and artisanal purposes. In the medieval era, walnut leaves were prized for their purported healing properties, used to treat ulcers, diarrhea, and skin conditions, while the husk and shell were employed in remedies for blood poisoning. Additionally, walnut leaves found use in fabric dyeing and leather tanning, indicating the tree's versatility.

By the 1830s, the walnut tree had established itself in the English wilderness, escaping cultivation to thrive in the natural environment. In Georgian garden design, walnut trees were strategically positioned to create visual interest, their majestic forms lending a sense of grandeur to the landscape. They were often planted in rows to form avenues or alleys, contributing to the formal symmetry and elegance characteristic of the era's gardens.

Today, the walnut tree is widely naturalized throughout England, particularly in lowland areas, where it can be found adorning hedgerows, property borders, and roadside landscapes.

Yew

TAXUS BACCATA

COMMON NAMES: ENGLISH YEW, COMMON YEW

The **yew** is a long-living evergreen shrub that can grow to over sixty feet tall if it is not trimmed and managed. Unlike other evergreens and conifers, the English yew doesn't bear its seed through a cone. Instead, the yew produces a berrylike encasement around the seed in a structure called an aril, which looks like a colorful husk or a thick rind.

The yew is one of the longest-living trees in Europe. Some of England's oldest yew trees are thought to be between two thousand and three thousand years old—and they look it. As it matures, the yew's trunk grows thick and fissured, giving it an almost ancient appearance.

MANSFIELD PARK

In *Mansfield Park*, Henry Crawford tells Edmund that he came across Thornton Lacey while riding. He lost his way after passing a familiar landmark: an old farmhouse surrounded by yew trees:

> "I told you I lost my way after passing that old farmhouse with the **yew-trees**, because I can never bear to ask; but I have not told you that, with my usual luck— for I never do wrong without gaining by it—I found myself in due time in the very place which I had a curiosity to see. I was suddenly, upon turning the corner of a steepish downy field, in the midst of a retired little village between gently rising hills; a small stream before me to be forded, a church standing on a sort of knoll to my right—which church was strikingly large and handsome for the place, and not a gentleman or half a gentleman's house to be seen excepting one—to be presumed the Parsonage—within a stone's throw of the said knoll and church. I found myself, in short, in Thornton Lacey."

SENSE AND SENSIBILITY

In *Sense and Sensibility*, Colonel Brandon's estate, Delaford Place, is described by Mrs. Jennings as picturesque, complete with an old yew arbor perfect for sitting and watching passersby on the road:

> "Delaford is a nice place, I can tell you . . . there is a dove-cote, some delightful stew-ponds, and a very pretty canal; and every thing, in short, that one could wish for; and, moreover, it is close to the church, and only a quarter of a mile from the turnpike-road, so 'tis never dull, for if you only go and sit up in an old **yew** arbour behind the house, you may see all the carriages that pass along."

A SHORT HISTORY OF YEW TREES

One of only three native conifers in England, yew trees often appear in old churchyards and other sacred spaces. While the reason for this isn't known, many believe that yews were planted around the graves of medieval plague victims to prevent sickness from seeping into the soil. Others suggest that churches and abbeys surrounded the graves of peasants with yew to keep the departed's livestock from grazing on the land. (Yew trees are incredibly toxic to animals.)

But the yew was associated with death and dying long before the Middle Ages. Yew branches were carried in funeral and Palm Sunday processions because of the tree's symbolic connection to immortality. After all, the yew can appear to return from the brink of decay, putting out new growth from a stem that looks as though it's been dead for years.

The yew's deep-green leaves and capacity to thrive in diverse forms and dimensions rendered it highly sought after in Regency garden layouts, especially within formal garden settings. Yews were often trimmed and shaped into dramatic-looking hedges and topiaries.

Still known as the "tree of the dead," the yew remains a symbol of immortality, partly due to its contemporary medicinal applications. The alkaloids in the tree are found in experimental anti-cancer drugs. The yew is also still used in landscaping worldwide, most often in the form of hedges.

CULTIVATING JANE

Shape a Boxwood Topiary

Shaping a topiary is a rewarding and artistic endeavor that can add classic elegance to any garden or landscape. In the grand gardens of Regency England, topiaries were revered for their uniqueness, adorning the landscapes of the parklands. Trees and shrubs like yew, holly, boxwood, and laurel were all used for creating topiaries—though boxwood is a good place to start for beginners. By crafting your own topiary, you can bring a touch of aristocratic charm to your modern garden.

Note: These steps can also apply to shrubs you already have in your garden.

YIELD: 1 TOPIARY

MATERIALS

Boxwood Plant (1)

Select a healthy, robust plant with dense foliage and a compact growth habit. Look for a sturdy central stem and well-defined branches. Avoid plants that show signs of a yellowing center, brown spots, or dark edges. (If your boxwood came from the nursery without a proper container, follow the potting instructions on page 143.)

Topiary Frame or Form (optional)

For more intricate topiary designs, consider using a topiary frame or form to guide your shaping process and achieve uniformity.

Gardening Gloves

Protect your hands from scratches and cuts while pruning and shaping the topiary with gardening gloves.

Garden Shears or Topiary Clippers

You'll need sharp pruning tools for trimming and shaping the topiary. Garden shears or topiary clippers are ideal for precision cutting.

Pruning Saw

A small pruning saw may be necessary for making larger cuts or removing thicker branches during the shaping process.

All-Purpose Fertilizer

While the boxwood is an evergreen, it differs from most evergreens in its nutritional needs. Typically, evergreens love acidic soil and need a fertilizer that provides that to their environment. However, boxwood does not thrive in acidic soil, so it needs an all-purpose plant food instead.

PLANT A BOXWOOD SHRUB IN A CONTAINER

Boxwood thrives in containers and can add a living sculpture to your existing garden space. To plant a boxwood shrub in a container, follow these easy steps:

1. CHOOSE CONTAINER

Select a pot at least twice the width of the root ball, and make sure it has a drainage hole! For additional drainage, layer gravel or broken pottery at the bottom.

2. PLANT SHRUB

Don your gardening gloves and fill the container halfway with potting mix. Remove the shrub from its nursery pot, gently loosen the roots, and position it in the container. Add more potting mix around the root ball, pressing gently, ensuring the top is an inch or two below the rim of the pot.

3. WATER AND MULCH

Water thoroughly, and add mulch to retain moisture, if needed. Place the container in partial to full sun, and keep the soil consistently moist but not waterlogged.

INSTRUCTIONS

1. CHOOSE TOPIARY STYLE

Decide on the desired shape and style of the topiary you want to create. Common shapes include cones, spheres, pyramids, spirals, or even whimsical animal forms. Consider the overall aesthetic of your garden and select a style that complements the surrounding landscape. If you're aiming for more elaborate topiary designs, consider using a topiary frame.

2. BEGIN SHAPING

Start by pruning the plant to remove dead, damaged, or overgrown branches. Use the saw for larger branches and shears for smaller ones. Then, begin shaping the plant into your desired form by carefully trimming away excess foliage. Start with the basic outline of your chosen shape and gradually refine the details as you progress.

3. TRIM REGULARLY

Regular maintenance is key to keeping your topiary looking neat and well defined. Trim new growth regularly to maintain the shape and size of your topiary, using sharp garden shears to make clean, precise cuts.

4. FERTILIZE AND WATER

Keep your topiary healthy and vibrant by regularly watering and fertilizing with all-purpose plant food during the growing season.

THE
HEDGEROW

Hedgerows are quintessential features of the English countryside and have long been celebrated for their ecological significance and cultural resonance. Dating back centuries, these linear green barriers serve many purposes, shaping the landscape and providing a habitat for a rich diversity of wildlife.

The origins of hedgerows in England can be traced back to ancient times, with some evidence suggesting their existence during the Roman period or even earlier. Initially established for practical purposes, such as creating boundaries, containing livestock, and providing shelter from the elements, hedgerows have evolved over the centuries into cherished features of the rural landscape.

During the Regency, hedgerows played a prominent role in the English countryside, serving the same practical and aesthetic purposes in the landscape. They continued to delineate boundaries between fields, estates, and properties. These living barriers provided a clear division of land ownership and prevented livestock from straying into neighboring fields or roads. Hedgerows were also essential for maintaining soil fertility and preventing erosion. Farmers relied on hedgerows as windbreaks to protect crops from strong winds and as natural barriers to retain soil moisture and nutrients. Landscape architects and garden designers used hedgerows to create striking vistas and frame views and provide sheltered pathways for leisurely strolls.

Today, hedgerows are renowned as biodiversity hotspots, providing food, shelter, and nesting sites for birds, mammals, butterflies, and other wildlife. Native plants thrive in the sheltered microclimates created by hedgerows, contributing to the overall richness and diversity of the ecosystem.

They also hold a special place in English culture and heritage, inspiring artists, poets, and writers throughout history. They are celebrated for their beauty and romantic charm, particularly when adorned with spring blossoms or autumn foliage. Many traditional English villages are bordered by ancient hedgerows, serving as living monuments to the country's rural heritage.

However, despite their ecological and cultural value, hedgerows face threats from agricultural intensification, urbanization, and neglect. The loss of hedgerows has led to habitat fragmentation and biodiversity decline, prompting conservation efforts to protect and restore these valuable habitats. Organizations such as Hedgelink advocate for the conservation of hedgerows and raise awareness of their importance.

CULTIVATING JANE

Make Dye from the Hedgerow

Using plants for natural dyeing is a time-honored craft that transforms fabric and yarn using colors extracted from plants found in the hedgerow. By collecting berries, leaves, flowers, and bark from plants such as elderberry, blackberry, nettle, and oak, you can create a palette of earthy tones and vibrant hues to color clothing or textiles.

This project works best when you modify it to your liking—feel free to adjust the measurements below! Use as much or as little fabric as you wish, and experiment with varying amounts of plant material to achieve different shades of dye.

YIELD: APPROXIMATELY 1 QUART OF DYE

MATERIALS

Fabric or Yarn (3 to 5 yards)

For best results, choose undyed natural fibers free of finishes or coatings, such as cotton, wool, or silk. These materials readily absorb natural dyes and produce vibrant colors.

Mordant (optional)

A mordant is a substance that helps fix the dye to the fabric or yarn and improves color-fastness. Common mordants include alum (for bright, clear colors), iron (for darker, more muted shades), and copper (for green tones). While optional, using a mordant can enhance the color intensity and longevity of the dyed material.

Plants (4 cups)

Choose berries, leaves, flowers, or bark from plants that produce dyes, such as elderberry, blackberry, nettle, or oak. Different plants yield different colors—for example, elderberry creates purples, and nettle makes a vibrant green—so experiment with combinations for unique shades! If you are foraging for your plants, be sure to collect sustainably and responsibly, leaving plenty behind for wildlife and others.

Stainless Steel or Enamel Pot

Use a pot dedicated to dyeing to avoid contamination with food or other substances. Stainless steel or enamel pots work well for heating the dye baths.

Water (5 quarts)

You'll need roughly four quarts of water to presoak your fabric or yarn, and one quart of water to extract the dye from the plant materials and create the dye bath. For best results, use clean, preferably distilled, water.

Strainer or Cheesecloth

These are used to strain the dye bath to remove plant particles and ensure a smooth dyeing process.

Gloves and Apron

Protect your clothing and skin from stains by wearing gloves and an apron while handling the dye materials.

Stirring Utensils

Use spoons or stirring rods to agitate the dye bath and distribute the dye evenly.

Sealable Containers

After extracting the dye from the plant materials, store the dye extracts in mason jars or other containers for future use. Label the containers to keep track of the dye sources and colors.

INSTRUCTIONS

1. **Presoak Fabric**

   Presoak your fabric or yarn in water to remove impurities and prepare the fibers to absorb the dye more evenly. You can also pretreat the fabric or yarn with a mordant, a chemical that helps the dye adhere more effectively and improves colorfastness, but this is optional. To ensure safety and effectiveness, be sure to follow recommended mordanting procedures carefully.

2. **Prepare Dye Extract**

   Place the plant material in a stainless steel or enamel pot and cover it with water. Bring the mixture to a boil, and then let it simmer for an hour or more, until the dye has been extracted from the plant material and the water has become the desired color. For deeper, richer colors, you may need to let the dye bath simmer for several hours or even overnight.

3. **Strain Dye Bath**

   Once the dye bath has reached the desired color intensity, it's time to put on your apron and gloves. Strain the plant material using a strainer or cheesecloth, leaving behind the liquid dye extract. You can compost the spent plant material or discard it in an eco-friendly manner.

4. **Dye Fabric or Yarn**

Submerge the presoaked fabric or yarn in the dye bath, ensuring it is fully immersed and evenly saturated. Simmer the fabric or yarn in the dye bath for at least an hour, stirring occasionally to promote even dye penetration. For lighter shades, you can reduce the dyeing time or dilute the dye bath with water.

5. **Rinse and Dry**

Once the fabric or yarn has achieved the desired color, remove it from the dye bath and rinse it thoroughly in cool water to remove excess dye. Hang the dyed material to dry in a well-ventilated area away from direct sunlight, taking care to avoid dripping on or staining other surfaces.

6. **Experiment and Enjoy**

Experiment with different plant materials, dye extraction methods, and mordants to create a range of colors and effects. Use your naturally dyed fabric and yarn to make clothing, textiles, and craft projects that reflect the beauty of the hedgerow and the artistry of natural dyeing. Store your dyes in a sealable container to use again.

JANE'S HEDGEROWS

Jane's descriptions of rural landscapes offer glimpses into the many kinds of hedgerows that would have been familiar to her. During the Regency, hedgerows were often mixed-species, wild boundaries that lined country lanes, but they could also be found as constructed, elegant landscape additions that adorned estate grounds. These types of hedgerows would have been familiar sights to Jane:

MIXED-SPECIES HEDGEROWS

The rural hedgerows of Regency England were often composed of a mix of native shrubs and trees, including hawthorn, blackthorn, elder, hazel, and dogwood. These mixed-species hedgerows created boundaries between fields and properties and provided vital habitats for wildlife.

HAWTHORN AND BLACKTHORN

Among the most common hedgerows in the Regency were those dominated by hawthorn and blackthorn. These old thorns would have been familiar to Jane, with their thorny branches and clusters of white flowers in spring.

BEECH HEDGEROWS

In more affluent areas or on estate lands, beech hedgerows, with their smooth gray bark and delicate green leaves that turn golden in autumn, added an air of elegance to the rural landscape.

PRIVET HEDGEROWS

In formal gardens or estate grounds, hedgerows were commonly created from privet, with glossy evergreen leaves and fragrant white flowers. While less common in the wild, privet hedgerows served as boundaries within more cultivated spaces.

Make Sloe Gin

Making sloe gin is a delightful and straightforward process requiring just a few ingredients and patience. Sloe gin is a traditional British liqueur made from sloes, the fruit of the blackthorn bush. The drupes are steeped in gin and sugar to create a rich, fruity, slightly tart beverage. The recipe is simple and can easily be made at home. Be prepared to wait, though—you'll have to let it sit for two months until it's ready to drink.

YIELD: APPROXIMATELY 25 OUNCES OF SLOE GIN

INGREDIENTS AND MATERIALS

Sloes (2 cups)

The blackthorn bush's small dark-purple fruits are typically harvested in late summer or early autumn, after the first frost has softened their skins. You can forage for sloes in hedgerows or, if you don't have access to a hedgerow, purchase them from a specialty food store.

Pricking Tool or Freezer

Sloe berries have tough skin, so you'll need to prick each drupe with a fork or toothpick—or freeze them before using to break down the cell walls and release its flavor.

Granulated Sugar (1 cup)

Granulated sugar is typically used to sweeten the sloe gin. The amount of sugar can be adjusted based on personal preference and the sweetness of the sloes.

Dry Gin (25.4 ounces, or "a fifth")

Choose a good-quality, neutral-flavored gin as the base for your sloe gin. The botanicals in the gin will complement the flavor of the sloes.

Glass Bottles with Airtight Lids (two 25.4-ounce bottles)

You'll need two clean, sterilized bottles—one in which to infuse the gin, and one to store the finished product. If you're in a pinch, you could sterilize and reuse the same bottle.

Muslin Cheesecloth or Fine-Mesh Sieve

After the sloes have infused in the gin, you'll need to strain the mixture to remove the solids using a muslin cloth or fine-mesh sieve.

Wide-Mouthed Pitcher

A wide-mouthed pitcher is a great option for catching the sloe gin while you're straining after the infusing process.

INSTRUCTIONS

1. **Prepare Berries**

   Rinse the sloes under cold water to remove any dirt or debris. Use a sharp knife or toothpick to prick each berry in several places, which will help release their juices during the steeping process. Alternatively, freeze the berries overnight before using them, as this can simulate the effect of frost and help break down their skins.

2. **Combine Ingredients**

   Place the prepared sloes in the sterilized bottle. Add the granulated sugar, then pour the gin over the berries and sugar. Seal the bottle tightly.

3. **Infuse**

   Store the bottle in a cool, dark place for at least two months, shaking it gently every few days to agitate the ingredients and help the flavors meld. The longer you leave the sloe gin to infuse, the more intense and complex the flavor will become. Some people steep their sloe gin for up to six months or longer for a richer, smoother taste.

4. **Strain and Bottle**

   After the desired steeping time has elapsed, strain the sloe gin through a fine-mesh sieve or muslin cheesecloth into a wide-mouthed pitcher. Discard the spent sloes and any solids. If desired, strain the sloe gin a second time for extra clarity. Then, pour the gin into a sterile bottle for keeping.

5. **Enjoy**

   Your homemade sloe gin is now ready to be enjoyed! Serve it neat or over ice, use it as a base for cocktails, or mix it with tonic water for a refreshing long drink. Sloe gin also makes a lovely gift for friends and family, especially during the holiday season.

6. **Store**

   Store your sloe gin in a cool, dark place away from direct sunlight, where it will keep indefinitely. Once opened, it's best consumed within a year for optimal flavor, although it will still be safe to drink beyond this time.

Apple

MALUS SPP.

Malus is a genus of small deciduous trees in the Rosaceae family, including domesti-cated **apples**, crab apples, and wild apples. The apple tree is small to medium sized, growing up to thirty feet tall but typically pruned down to a smaller, more manageable size. Fruits develop over the summer and early fall, and, depending on the variety, they can vary from large, green, and sour to red, small, and sweet.

The domestic apple tree should not be confused with the crab apple, which is native to England. The crab apple fruits are much smaller than the domestic apple, but hybrid varieties have been bred to combine characteristics from both species.

EMMA

Miss Bates rambles about getting apples as a gift from Mr. Knightley:

> "The **apples** themselves are the very finest sort for baking, beyond a doubt; all from Donwell—some of Mr. Knightley's most liberal supply. He sends us a sack every year; and certainly there never was such a keeping **apple** anywhere as one of his trees—I believe there is two of them. My mother says the orchard was always famous in her younger days."

Given in the winter, these apples would likely have been a Lemon Pippin or Warner's King variety. The Lemon Pippin was first recorded in the eighteenth century but is thought to be much older. The apple sweetens the longer it is stored, which makes it a wonderful option for winter treats and baked goods. The Warner's King is an equally old variety, but whereas the Lemon Pippin is tiny and yellow, the Warner's King is large, firm, and green:

NORTHANGER ABBEY

Catherine visits Henry's parsonage at Woodston, where the cottage is nestled in a grove of trees, which includes apple trees:

> "Well, if it was my house, I would never sit anywhere else. Oh! what a sweet little cottage there is among the trees—**apple trees** too! It is the prettiest cottage!"

Jane writes that Northanger Abbey is thirty miles from Bath, or, one could interpret, somewhere in Somerset. Locally understood, it's possible that those apple trees at Woodston could have been a handful of varieties: Court of Wick, Golden Knob, Bridgwater Pippin, Hoary Morning, and Tom Putt were all varieties grown in Somerset at the time.

PERSUASION

Well into the narrative of *Persuasion*, Mr. Shepherd discusses the travesty of stolen apples with Captain Wentworth's brother, Edward:

"Bless me! how very odd! I shall forget my own name soon, I suppose. A name that I am so very well acquainted with; knew the gentleman so well by sight; seen him a hundred times; came to consult me once, I remember, about a trespass of one of his neighbours; farmer's man breaking into his orchard; wall torn down; **apples** *stolen; caught in the fact; and afterwards, contrary to my judgement, submitted to an amicable compromise. Very odd indeed!"*

Again, Somerset being the main locale where the country houses of Somersetshire, Lyme Regis, and Bath are set, the apple choices would have been like those in *Emma.*

A SHORT HISTORY OF APPLES

The domestic apple is descended from the ancient *Malus sieversii* apple tree, native to the Tian Shan mountains in Kazakhstan. It was the Romans who started grafting different varieties of apple trees together to get better-tasting fruit. When Julius Caesar came to England in 55 BC, domesticated apples came along with him. Then, in the seventeenth century, colonists brought apples across the ocean to North America.

During the Georgian era, apples were mainly used for baking and cider-making. The fruit was a valuable source of food, and the trees could easily be found in private gardens, orchards, and even in city gardens. In the garden, apple trees were highly sought after because of their delicate white and pink blooms and gem-colored fruits. The trees could be trained to grow in specific shapes, like an espalier, to create points of interest in any garden.

In England, apples can still be found all over the countryside. Trees of all varieties have naturalized and often grow wild in hedgerows and along roadsides, which makes for a fun harvest time if you don't have apple trees of your own. Thousands of varieties of apple trees and fruits can be found globally year-round, both at the market and in plant nurseries.

Beech

FAGUS SYLVATICA

COMMON NAMES: COMMON BEECH, EUROPEAN BEECH

The **beech** creates a dense canopy, shading the ground beneath so completely that little can grow at its base. In summer, the tree has bright, almost neon-green leaves that, in fall, turn gold and bronze. It produces a prickly-husked fruit called the beechnut, which is edible and can be used to make oil, coffee substitute, and flour for baking.

MANSFIELD PARK

The beech tree is referenced in *Mansfield Park* as the entire crew, including the Crawfords, Fanny, and Edmund, make their way across the lawn toward the terrace and the wilderness, which Jane describes as "chiefly of larch and laurel, and **beech** cut down." (See page 112 for the full excerpt.)

By "beech cut down," Jane means that the beech hedges on either side of the walk have been trimmed.

A SHORT HISTORY OF BEECH TREES

The beechnut has been a staple food in England and western Europe since ancient times. It offers a reliable source of energy during the fall and winter months when fresh produce is scarce.

In addition to their culinary use, beech trees were also valued for their ornamental qualities. They were often used to create privacy fences, walkways, and alleys in woodland gardens, particularly during the Regency era. The beech tree's towering stature and elegant appearance made it a top choice for avenues and a common focal point in parks, gardens, and tall hedgerows.

The dense canopy of beech trees provides a habitat for various rare plant species, including different types of bitter cress and terrestrial orchids, which thrive in the sheltered environment beneath the tree. Beyond its role in the ecosystem, beechwood remains highly versatile and is still utilized in various applications today due to its hardness. It is commonly used for smoking meat, crafting furniture, and manufacturing tools.

Elder

SAMBUCUS NIGRA

COMMON NAMES: BLACK ELDER, EUROPEAN ELDERBERRY

At full maturity, a black **elder** tree can grow to thirty feet and can be identified by its serrated, feather-shaped leaves that turn shades of yellow and purple in the autumn. In the spring, the tree blooms with clusters of fragrant white flowers. Once pollinated, small black fruits develop in late summer and early fall. Of the two most common elder varieties in the United Kingdom, the black elder (*Sambucus nigra*) was favored in Georgian-era garden design:

EMMA

In *Emma*, Harriet and Emma are traveling in their carriage, having just learned that Frank Churchill will finally be coming for a visit.

*Emma's spirits were mounted quite up to happiness: every thing wore a different air; James and his horses seemed not half so sluggish as before. When she looked at the hedges, she thought the **elder** at least must soon be coming out; and when she turned round to Harriet, she saw something like a look of spring, a tender smile even there.*

A SHORT HISTORY OF ELDER TREES

The elder tree has long been prized for its versatile uses, both culinary and practical. Its flowers have historically been utilized to create teas, wines, liqueurs, and baked goods, while various parts of the tree have been employed in dye-making, historically for the production of Harris Tweed in the Outer Hebrides of Scotland. The bark yields gray and black dyes, the berries offer blue and purple hues, and the leaves create yellow and green tones.

In the realm of Regency garden design, the elder tree played a significant role in shaping hedgerows and shrubberies. Its tendency to produce offshoots and form dense masses made it ideal for natural garden layouts, providing structure and dimension with its dense foliage. Often situated along garden borders, elder trees added texture and color to otherwise plain areas. During Jane Austen's era, elderberries and flowers retained medicinal importance, commonly used to treat colds and various strains of flu.

Today, the black elder thrives in temperate regions worldwide, particularly in England, where it flourishes in habitats ranging from wild woodlands to roadside hedgerows and cultivated gardens. Its popularity in modern garden design stems from its small size and aesthetic impact, with cultivators leveraging its foliage, flowers, and fruit to create striking visual displays.

Elm

ULMUS MINOR 'ATINIA'

COMMON NAMES: FIELD ELM, COMMON ELM, ENGLISH ELM, HORSE MAY

The English **elm** can live over one hundred years and grow to over one hundred feet. It is known to be one of the fastest-growing trees in Europe, which makes it a solid option for those who wish to plant a tree that will grow tall during their lifetime.

EMMA

In *Emma*, elms shade the path near Highbury. Emma and Harriet are approached by a group of strangers as they walk into the grove of trees:

*About half a mile beyond Highbury, making a sudden turn, and deeply shaded by **elms** on each side, it became for a considerable stretch very retired; and when the young ladies had advanced some way into it, they had suddenly perceived at a small distance before them, on a broader patch of greensward by the side, a party of gipsies.*

A SHORT HISTORY OF ELM TREES

Despite its moniker, the English elm likely did not originate in England but is believed to have been introduced by Romans through their trade routes. Nonetheless, it thrived in the English landscape, quickly becoming a beloved fixture. Renowned for its rapid growth, towering stature, and stunning foliage, the English elm was a favored choice during the Georgian era for adorning parks, gardens, and avenues, where its presence dominated the scenery and provided ample shade for leisurely picnics and strolls.

During this period, the English elm played a significant role in shaping the aesthetic of the English countryside, contributing to the picturesque landscapes that defined the era. Its graceful form and verdant canopy became emblematic of the idyllic pastoral scenes depicted in art and literature of the time.

However, the golden age of the English elm was not to last. The devastating outbreak of Dutch elm disease in the 1970s wreaked havoc on the European elm population, decimating vast swaths of trees across the continent. In the United Kingdom alone, more than twenty-five million trees fell victim to this deadly pathogen, including a substantial portion of the English elm population.

The impact of Dutch elm disease was particularly severe, leading to a significant decline in the prevalence of English elms in the wild. Today, sightings of this once ubiquitous tree are rare, relegated to occasional appearances in isolated woodlands and hedgerows. Despite its diminished presence, the legacy of the English elm endures, as a reminder of a bygone era when its majestic form graced the English countryside, casting its shade over generations of admirers.

Gooseberry

RIBES UVA-CRISPA

COMMON NAME: EUROPEAN GOOSEBERRY

The European **gooseberry** is a small, prickly bush in the Rosaceae family that is sought after for its fruit by the same name. It's also closely related to other plants in the *Ribes* genus, like red and black currants. The bush itself grows five feet tall and no wider than six feet. Gooseberries are generally ready for harvest in mid-spring, depending on the weather. The European gooseberry is larger than a grape but smaller than a plum and can be found in shades of green and yellow.

MANSFIELD PARK

When Fanny Price first arrives at Mansfield Park, Mrs. Bertram offers her a gooseberry tart in a failed attempt to make her feel better:

> *. . . and her consciousness of misery was therefore increased by the idea of its being a wicked thing for her not to be happy. The fatigue, too, of so long a journey, became soon no trifling evil. In vain were the well-meant condescensions of Sir*

*Thomas, and all the officious prognostications of Mrs. Norris that she would be a good girl; in vain did Lady Bertram smile and make her sit on the sofa with herself and pug, and vain was even the sight of a **gooseberry** tart towards giving her comfort; she could scarcely swallow two mouthfuls before tears interrupted her, and sleep seeming to be her likeliest friend, she was taken to finish her sorrows in bed.*

A SHORT HISTORY OF GOOSEBERRIES

European gooseberries, native to Europe, western Asia, and northern Africa, boast a rich history deeply intertwined with England's landscape and culinary traditions. Cultivated for centuries, the distinction between native wild bushes and garden escapees has become blurred over time due to their long-standing presence in English gardens. Valued for their medicinal properties during the Middle Ages, gooseberries gradually gained popularity as a common food choice in subsequent centuries.

During the Regency era, gooseberries soared in popularity as dessert delicacies, captivating the palates and imaginations of many. Their renown was such that gooseberry clubs emerged across England, fostering a culture of competition and camaraderie among enthusiasts vying to grow the largest and most flavorful fruit.

The peculiar name "gooseberry" itself adds an intriguing layer to its history. Though the theory is unsubstantiated, a folktale suggests that the name originates from the use of the tart fruit in goose dishes. The fruit's tartness complemented the rich flavors of roasted goose, hence the association.

In England today, gooseberries can still be discovered thriving in hedgerows and woodlands, particularly around more established homes and communities. Although not commonly found in markets, dedicated gooseberry aficionados maintain clandestine bushes, returning each year to harvest their prized berries and ensuring the tradition of gooseberry gathering persists.

Honeysuckle

LONICERA PERICLYMENUM

COMMON NAMES: COMMON HONEYSUCKLE, WOODBINE

Honeysuckle is a vining, fast-growing bush that perennially produces fragrant trumpet-shaped flowers. Its oval-shaped leaves are a deep shade of green and appear opposite each other along the plant's stem.

The flowers emerge in the middle of summer and can vary in shade from cream to yellow to orange. As the season continues, many blooms get a smattering of blush color along their edges. The flowers produce a sweet, delicious nectar that draws in many pollinators. In the autumn, they give way to red berries, which are quickly fed upon by birds and other wildlife.

While many species of honeysuckle have been introduced to England over the years and become naturalized and invasive, *Lonicera periclymenum* is a true native.

SENSE AND SENSIBILITY

Jane describes the exterior of Barton Cottage in *Sense and Sensibility* as lacking desirable physical attributes that would make the cottage a comfortable home for the family:

> *As a house, Barton Cottage, though small, was comfortable and compact; but as a cottage it was defective, for the building was regular, the roof was tiled, the window shutters were not painted green, nor were the walls covered with **honeysuckles**.*

Though modern gardening and landscape design can label honeysuckle as an invasive weed in many parts of the world, honeysuckle was much desired during Jane's time and would have been a welcome and charming sight.

A SHORT HISTORY OF HONEYSUCKLE

The honeysuckle vine has long been prevalent in the woodlands and wilderness of England. The name "honeysuckle" is believed to have emerged from the tradition of picking the flowers and "sucking" the mound of nectar from the narrow end of the bloom.

Honeysuckle's other common name, woodbine, refers to the plant's habit of weaving its way up trunks and around limbs, causing trees to appear twisted. These trunks and limbs were used to make visually stunning walking sticks, often used in the eighteenth and nineteenth centuries by respected members of communities.

Georgian landscape and garden designers loved honeysuckle for its sweet fragrance, delicate flowers, and radical climbing habit. Often trained to grow over trellises, arches, and walls, honeysuckle contributed a lush beauty to many gardens.

Today, honeysuckle can still be found in countless gardens, woodlands, hedgerows, and wildernesses all over England. It can be seen creeping over trees and other shrubs and is still sold each year at plant nurseries. Many cultivars are available with different-colored flowers and growing habits. Honeysuckle is also frequently used in floral design, and the essence from its edible blooms makes a tasty addition to many cordials, desserts, and flavored sugars.

Nettles, Thistles, Heather

NETTLE

URTICA DIOICA

COMMON NAMES: COMMON NETTLE, STINGING NETTLE

Native **nettle** can be found all over the English countryside. It is identified by its serrated green leaves. Often found growing in the understory of wooded environments or in meadows that have previously been used as farmland, it thrives in rich ground that retains moisture. The stems and undersides of the leaves of the stinging nettle are lined with hollow hairs that transfer histamine and other chemicals onto the skin if touched, producing a burning sensation. This genetic mutation keeps the plant from being eaten in its raw state.

THISTLE

CARDUUS SPP., *CIRSIUM* SPP.

COMMON NAMES: CREEPING THISTLE, SPEAR THISTLE, MARSH THISTLE,
STEMLESS THISTLE, WOOLY THISTLE, MUSK THISTLE

Thistle belongs to the daisy family, Asteraceae, and there are two main genera of thistles that are native to England: *Cirsium* and *Carduus*. The thistle has prickly spines on its stems and leaves to protect the plant from being disturbed or eaten. It produces flower heads made of individual flowers that go to seed in the fall and float away in the wind or on an animal's fur. Thistle seeds are also a primary source of food for many birds, including the goldfinch.

HEATHER

ERICA SPP., *CALLUNA VULGARIS*

COMMON NAMES: CROSS-LEAVED HEATH, BELL HEATHER, COMMON HEATHER,
LING, TWISTED HEATH

Native **heather** is an iconic sight across Britain and a reference folded into works by Austen and the Brontës. Three widespread species can easily be found in England. Bell heather, cross-leaved heather, and ling heather often grow close to each other, even though ling and bell heather prefer drier ground and cross-leaved heath grows best in damp soil:

Bell heather, twisted heath *(Erica cinerea)*: Bell heather has needlelike leaves and a completely smooth stem. The plant produces deep-purple flowers on spikes.

Cross-leaved heath *(Erica tetralix)*: Like bell heather, cross-leaved heath has tiny needlelike leaves but a hairy stem. It produces pink flowers that appear at the tops of the stems.

Ling heather, common heather (*Calluna vulgaris*): Look for little scaly leaves and a smoother stem than cross-leaved heath. Ling heather produces spikes of lavender-colored flowers.

All three species thrive in sandy, nutrient-poor soil but need complete exposure to the elements. Any interference from shrubs or trees and heather will struggle to live.

SENSE AND SENSIBILITY

As Elinor and Edward Ferrars take a stroll through the park surrounding Mr. Jennings's estate in the English countryside, Edward describes his taste in landscapes, revealing his practical and unromantic nature:

> "*I like a fine prospect, but not on picturesque principles. I do not like crooked, twisted, blasted trees. I admire them much more if they are tall, straight, and flourishing. I do not like ruined, tattered cottages. I am not fond of **nettles** or **thistles**, or **heath** blossoms.*"

Jane likely lumped heather in with nettles and thistle because of its prickly texture, which could snag skirts and irritate bare ankles or feet.

MANSFIELD PARK

During a walk in the gardens of Mansfield Park, Fanny Price and her cousin Mary Crawford encounter the gardener, who has recently been advised by Mary on the illness of his grandson. Here, he shows his appreciation of Mary by sharing his knowledge of plants with her:

> *. . . since Julia's leaving them they had been met by the gardener, with whom she had made a most satisfactory acquaintance, for she had set him right as to his grandson's illness, convinced him that it was an ague, and promised him a charm for it; and he, in return, had shown her all his choicest nursery of plants, and actually presented her with a very curious specimen of **heath**.*

A SHORT HISTORY OF NATIVE NETTLE, THISTLE, AND HEATHER

Nettles have a storied history in England. In ancient times, they were valued for their medicinal properties and used to treat various ailments, such as arthritis, allergies, and skin conditions. Nettles were also a common food source, particularly during times of famine. They were blanched, cleaned, and then added to soups, made into teas, and eaten as a vegetable. There were even periods of history when nettles were grown for their fibers, which were spun into cloth similar to linen. Today, nettles are still widely found throughout England, often growing in damp, nutrient-rich soil.

While appreciated for its beauty and as a food source for pollinators, thistle can act as an invasive weed, aggravating farmers and gardeners. Even the smallest remaining roots ensure that the plant will appear again the following season, and one musk thistle pod can release more than one hundred thousand seeds! Thistle is extremely common throughout the United Kingdom and is the national symbol and flower of Scotland.

Heather holds a special place in the culture and folklore of England, where it blankets the landscape of the moorlands with a sea of purple blooms in late summer. Heather is essential to several traditional crafts, such as basket weaving and thatching. Centuries of medicinal use indicate its value in healing a variety of ailments, from arthritis to sleep disorders. In addition to its practical uses, heather holds symbolic significance in English literature and folklore, representing the wild and untamed beauty of the countryside. Today, heather thrives in England's upland areas, providing a habitat for wildlife and coloring the classic moorland landscape with pinks, purples, and greens.

Afternote

CELEBRATING NATURE THROUGH JANE AUSTEN'S NOVELS

As we conclude our journey through Jane Austen's garden of stories, it's clear that nature isn't only a backdrop in Jane's novels—it's a character in its own right. From the blooming roses at Mansfield Park to the wild tangles of greenery in *Emma*'s Highbury, Jane's stories are filled with lush gardens and diverse parklands that speak volumes about her characters and their worlds. Roses are symbols of purity and innocence, reflecting the moral fiber of characters like Fanny Price. And those strawberries in *Emma*? They're a reminder of class and humility in a world of flashy displays and social climbers. After all, the plants aren't mere decoration. They're part of the social fabric, too.

By delving into Jane's descriptions of plants, we're not just getting a glimpse into Regency-era England—we're also learning about our own relationship with nature and how it shapes society. If we recognize the enduring significance of nature in both literature and life, we can appreciate the beauty and symbolism of plants in literature and draw inspiration from their portrayal in storytelling.

Jane's novels serve as a reminder of the interconnectedness between humans and the natural world. We are encouraged to cultivate a deeper appreciation for nature's role in shaping society and reminding us of how horticulture and nature have changed over time through the lens of human intervention.

So, as we say goodbye, let's take a moment to appreciate the beauty and significance of the natural world in both literature and life. When we're wandering through our gardens or getting lost in a novel, let's remember that nature isn't just something to look at—it's something to celebrate, cherish, and protect.

REGENCY HORTICULTURAL LANGUAGE: A GLOSSARY

FLOWER-BED

Flower-beds, typical of the Regency era, were areas cultivated for growing flowers, shrubs, vegetables, fruits, or herbs and maintained a sense of deliberate arrangement. They often included smaller edging plants at the front, medium-sized shrubs in the middle, and larger, more eye-catching plants at the back.

FLOWER GARDEN

A flower garden is a dedicated space for cultivating flowering plants. During the Regency era, flower gardens were known for their formal designs, emphasizing symmetry, order, and geometric shapes. They featured parterres (elaborate garden beds arranged with low hedges) gravel paths, and vibrant flowers. Topiaries, plants shaped like animals or people, were another distinctive element. Water fountains, statues, and garden ornaments were commonly incorporated into Regency flower gardens.

GARDEN

A garden serves as a deliberately arranged outdoor area for cultivating particular plants. During the Regency period, gardens represented humanity's dominance over nature. Primarily designed for aesthetic pleasure, the formal gardens of grand residences differed from their surrounding parklands. These formal gardens reflected the wealth and social ambitions of each family. While lower- and middle-class families cultivated gardens for sustenance and livestock, the affluent showcased their prosperity and refined preferences through a variety of gardens, ranging from kitchen and pleasure gardens to expansive grounds.

GARDENER

The intricate landscape designs of the Regency era demanded extensive upkeep. Prominent estates such as the fictional Pemberley and Northanger Abbey in Jane's novels would have employed sizable staff to maintain the grounds.

Large estates typically hired from fifty to over a hundred gardeners, comprising full-time, year-round employees and seasonal staff for spring, summer, and fall. The pivotal role of the master gardener involved planning and organizing the maintenance and cultivation of every plant on the estate. The master gardener's team included apprentices and assistants, many of whom entered the profession at a young age. Gardeners often moved between estates, advancing through the ranks to gain experience.

GRAVEL WALK

In Regency landscape design, the gravel walk emerged as a crucial element, its composition varying based on garden style and purpose. While paths were sometimes crafted from shells, brick, or packed dirt, gravel stood out as the favored option due to its low maintenance. Gravel walks required no regular watering, mowing, or weeding, offering easy upkeep with a simple rake.

These paths, typically meandering through shrubbery, were bordered by low hedges or flower-beds, dividing garden areas and connecting different sections. For instance, a gravel walk might link a walled garden to an open lawn.

Beyond practicality, gravel walks also kept feet and dresses dry, ensuring the ladies of the estate remained above the damp grass. In the literature of the Regency and Georgian eras, particularly in Jane's novels, straying from the gravel walk by the shrubbery signaled a disturbance in the character or plot. In her novels, Jane often utilized gravel walks as settings for significant events and conversations, highlighting social status and class distinctions within the paths.

GREENHOUSE

A greenhouse is a transparent structure for year-round plant cultivation that maintains a regulated temperature. It revolutionized the cultivation of tropical and temperate plants, allowing delicate plants to thrive.

The term "hothouse" is often used interchangeably with "greenhouse," but with a potential difference. A greenhouse can fluctuate in temperature with the seasons, acting as a hothouse in winter. In contrast, a hothouse maintains a constant warm temperature year-round, providing a more controlled environment. In their early days, hothouses, like the one at Chelsea Physic Garden in London (constructed in 1681), faced challenges and high costs. The improved mechanics and materials of the eighteenth century made heated greenhouses more common, particularly among wealthy plant collectors.

GROUNDS

In the Regency era, an estate's grounds—encompassing open areas not occupied by structures—held significance for landowners. Impressions mattered, so the approach to the house often meandered through well-curated landscapes, showcasing its best attributes. These grounds boasted winding pathways, expansive fields, and water features, like rivers and lakes. Controlled wildlife, such as deer herds and livestock, freely roamed, contributing to an estate's charm. Groundskeepers and gardeners maintained ornamental gardens, lawns, and the wilderness. The extent of an estate's grounds varied based on the family's wealth and land size.

HA-HA

The ha ha, also known as a sunken fence, blind fence, or deer wall, emerged in the eighteenth century as a landscape feature. It serves as a vertical barrier for free-roaming animals while preserving scenic views. The design includes a sloping lawn meeting a retaining wall, which is sunk into the ground, creating the illusion that there is no drop-off at all. Common in major estates during the Georgian era, ha-has were crucial for achieving picturesque views without artificial-looking fences.

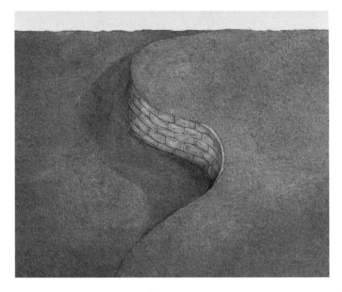

Before the mechanical lawnmower's invention, maintaining a trimmed lawn relied on allowing livestock to graze. The ha-ha prevented animals from approaching too closely and disrupting formal gardens and lawns.

The name's origin is thought to come from the exclamations of surprise ("ha! ha!") that people would make upon encountering the hidden fence. The feature was designed to be invisible from a distance, creating an element of surprise when visitors realized there was a sudden drop in the ground.

KITCHEN GARDEN

A Regency kitchen garden, essential for estates during the Georgian era, was distinct from ornamental gardens. Positioned near the house for convenience, it was often walled or fenced to safeguard plants. Smaller properties, like Jane's Chawton home, simply integrated edible plants into ornamental gardens. Larger estates featured expansive kitchen gardens with year-round production, equipped with greenhouses, cold frames, exposed raised beds, and fruit orchards.

LAWN

Regency estates highly valued their extensive lawns, which served as spaces for leisure activities, such as strolling, shuttlecock, and lawn bowling, in good weather. These vast lawns required regular upkeep. Gardeners, often working in large teams during the morning dew, used scythes—typically employed for cutting grain—to shear the grass with a low, repetitive motion. To ensure well-defined edges, sheep-shearing clippers were used as part of the weekly maintenance routine.

The daisy grubber, resembling an angled pick, was used to remove weeds from the lawn, leaving the grass and soil largely undisturbed. Additionally, grazing livestock, kept away from the formal gardens by ha-has, contributed to managing the expansive lawns of massive estates.

NURSERYMEN

Nurserymen were pivotal figures in Regency horticulture, introducing new plant species and varieties to the upper echelons of gardening. Specializing in specific plant types or families, they managed hothouses, greenhouses, and retail shops, catering to a diverse clientele, from the general public to public gardens and the head gardeners of opulent estates. Some even served as consultants for large estates, contributing to garden planning and specific plant supplies.

The Georgian period was a significant one for collectors without personal plant hunters. Finally, plant nurseries across England expanded their collections from vegetables to various perennials, including temperate and tropical species brought back from afar by their own plant hunters—which required hothouses. During this time, retail greenhouses began offering plant rental services, enabling individuals to portray the ambiance of an affluent estate. The presence of indoor plants became crucial for those aspiring to be part of high society.

OLD THORNS

During the Regency era in England, thorn trees, like the hawthorn (*Crataegus monogyna*), also known as the May tree, served multiple decorative and practical functions and were frequently referred to as "old thorns." Exploding with delightful white or pink blossoms in spring and bearing autumn fruit, called haws, hawthorns were commonly used for hedgerows and property delineation due to their dense foliage and thorny branches, making them well suited for livestock containment. Another common thorn tree was the blackthorn (*Prunus spinosa*), recognized for its dark, thorny branches and small white flowers. Blackthorns were also favored for hedgerows and property boundaries, and their dark-blue sloes gained fame for their use in gin production.

Additional thorny trees and bushes, such as the wild rose, crab apple, and dogwood, were valued for their aesthetic appeal and practical utility in English landscape design during Jane's era. Her vivid descriptions of these thorn trees in her novels provide a realistic glimpse into the charming English landscapes she cherished.

PARKS

Regency estates, including those mentioned in Jane's novels, were often called "parks." Unlike the contemporary understanding of a park as green space for public enjoyment, the parks of Jane's time were primarily deer parks. These deer parks, called simply "parks" during that period, were typically royal investments and required grants from the monarchy for construction. Invitation-only, these parks served as exclusive hunting and sporting grounds.

Functioning as status symbols and sources of timber, deer parks traced their origins back to the Middle Ages. Despite their expansiveness, these parks were enclosed and surrounded by ha-has and thick rows of trees marking the property line. Maintaining such vast areas was expensive and time-consuming, demanding a substantial team of gardeners.

These parks served as venues for leisurely walks and picnics on large estate grounds, and they were utilized for hunting, a favored pastime among the upper classes during the Regency, which involved hounds and horses in pursuit of deer.

PINERY

A pinery is a specialized hothouse designed for cultivating pineapple plants and their fruit. Featuring pitched roofs for optimal light exposure and temperature control, these structures also facilitated the accumulation of necessary moisture for the extended growth cycle of pineapples. Incorporating a heating element ensured a consistently warm environment throughout all seasons.

PLEASURE GROUNDS

Pleasure grounds in the Regency era were decorative outdoor areas near the estate house that were primarily enjoyed by the residents, especially women. These spaces featured wooded paths, gravel walks through shrubberies, plant conservatories, and flower-beds—providing a secure environment for strolls in nature suitable for the ladies of that time. Typically enclosed by terraces and ha-has, these grounds incorporated rustic seating, hidden elements, and additions such as temples, artificial ruins, and water features.

SUCCESSION HOUSE

A succession house, characteristic of the Regency-era estate, was an enclosed greenhouse for nurturing young plants. As the plants matured and gained the strength to thrive outdoors, they were replaced by new ones in a continuous cycle.

SHRUBBERY

The term "shrubbery" is often misunderstood as a singular shrub or a few shrub plants, but this interpretation is technically incorrect when referring to the Regency era. In the Georgian period, a shrubbery was a singular park or garden where numerous shrubs, trees, and flower species were closely planted in a specific manner.

In the formal pleasure gardens of an estate, the shrubbery was highly valued and emblematic of the picturesque style prevalent during Jane's time. This style emphasized individual plants and the aesthetic they collectively created, aiming for a natural appearance. Shrubberies were typically designed as winding gravel walks. These walks were broad enough for two or even three people to walk side by side, leading through the pleasure grounds to various viewpoints and discoveries before circling back to the house. The layout of shrubberies often formed a larger circular walk, guiding visitors to specific destinations, such as the greenhouse, orchard, temple, or stable. The intention was to guide individuals through points of interest scattered along the way.

The shrubbery provided a refuge for women like Jane's heroines, who could escape with friends or a beau or enjoy solitude without requiring an escort. It was considered a safe space for women to wander alone.

Within a shrubbery, plants were tiered, with shorter plants near the path's edge, followed by medium-sized flowering plants and shrubs, and finally, trees at the back.

Shrubberies took various forms, from closed, enclosing both sides of the walk that would open up to planned vistas, to completely open, where only one side was planted.

WILDERNESS

In larger estate grounds, the transitional zone between formal gardens and the surrounding park was called "the wilderness" during the Regency era. Despite its name, the wilderness was as carefully planned as the rest of the estate, featuring sporadic and free-flowing plantings, native trees, grasses, ponds, waterfalls, and meadow-like lawns. Maintaining uninterrupted views was crucial, leading to instances where mature trees, structures, or cottages were relocated for the perfect vista. The design of each estate's wilderness was meticulous and tailored to the regional topography, incorporating walking paths and private seating areas.

Acknowledgments

I am fortunate to have an extraordinary team of individuals beside me who have contributed their expertise and support to make this book a reality. At the risk of sounding cliché, these people have nurtured my ideas, pruned my prose, watered my imagination, and allowed this work to flourish.

Laura Mazer, my extraordinary agent, you have supported me from the beginning. Your insights, industry knowledge, and tireless efforts have propelled this book from idea to reality. Thank you for championing my work and helping it find its place in the literary landscape. You always help me find my way.

To Andrews McMeel, the publisher who took a leap of faith in this unique project, thank you for recognizing the potential of combining the beauty of Jane's prose with the allure of the horticultural world.

Melissa Rhodes Zahorsky, my brilliant editor, you possess a keen eye for detail and an uncanny ability to push me just a little bit further. Your insightful feedback and tireless dedication have polished this work. Thank you for believing in me.

Jessica Roux, the enchanting illustrator whose work has breathed life into the pages of this book, your artistic talent has transformed my words in ways I never thought were possible. You have made this book a feast for the eyes, and I am deeply grateful for your imaginative collaboration.

Rachel Ramsey, your intellect and passion for Jane's works have been an inspiration throughout this journey. Your scholarly guidance and thought-provoking questions have helped this project more than you'll ever know. Thank you!

Emma Yandle at Chawton House and Lizzie Dunford at the Jane Austen's House museum, your knowledge, generosity, and access to historical resources have enriched the authenticity of this book. Your collaboration has allowed readers to step into the verdant wilderness that shaped Jane's imagination, and for that, I am deeply grateful.

To Mom and Dad, my original support system, thank you for sowing the seeds of curiosity in me, nurturing my love for literature and horticulture, and always letting me read at the supper table.

Maddie and Liv, my delightful cherubs who couldn't care less about plants, thank you for bringing laughter and joy into my days—and for making me a mom. May you always find inspiration in the most unlikely places.

Jenn, you are my companion and the sunshine that nourishes my creative spirit. Your unwavering belief in me and your love-infused encouragement have sustained me throughout this project. Thank you for always giving me a shoulder to cry on—both in happiness and in despair brought on by procrastination.

To all the friends, family, and loved ones who have offered encouragement and support, thank you for always being there. Your belief in my writing ability has been a constant source of inspiration.

And to the readers who have wandered with me through the shrubberies and wildernesses of Jane's world: I wouldn't be here without you.

ABOUT THE AUTHOR

Molly Williams is the author of *The Junior Plant Lover's Handbook: A Green-Thumb Guide for Kids*; *How to Speak Flower: A Kid's Guide to Buds, Blooms, and Blossoms*; *Taming the Potted Beast: The Strange and Sensational History of the Not-So-Humble Houseplant*; and *Killer Plants: Growing and Caring for Flytraps, Pitcher Plants, and Other Deadly Flora*. Molly lives in New England with her wife and children but spends ample time on her family's farm in southern Illinois, where she was raised. She is an avid houseplant collector, gardener, florist, and teacher of many things, including writing.

ABOUT THE ILLUSTRATOR

Jessica Roux is a bestselling illustrator, author, and gardener based just outside of Nashville, Tennessee. She loves exploring in her own backyard and being surrounded by an abundance of nature. Using subdued colors and rhythmic shapes, she renders flora and fauna with intricate detail reminiscent of old-world beauty. Jessica is the author and illustrator of *Floriography: An Illustrated Guide to the Victorian Language of Flowers*, the Woodland Wardens Oracle Deck & Guidebook, and *Ornithography: An Illustrated Guide to Bird Lore & Symbolism*. She has also illustrated several children's books, including the *New York Times* bestseller *The Wheel of the Year: An Illustrated Guide to Nature's Rhythms*.